THOMAS JEFFERSON'S
EUROPEAN
TRAVEL DIARIES

Edited by
James McGrath Morris
&
Persephone Weene

Introduction by
Dean M. Sagar

with Illustrations by the author
adapted by Betsy Bayley

Isidore Stephanus Sons, Publishing
Ithaca, New York

Designed by Betsy Bayley
Typesetting by Giles Bayley
Illustrations adapted by Betsy Bayley

Introduction Copyright ©1987 by
Dean M. Sagar
Text Copyright ©1987 by
James McGrath Morris

E
332.745
.J44
1987

R00601 02600

Address inquires to:
Isidore Stephanus Sons, Publishing
P.O. Box 6772
Ithaca, New York 14851-6772

Printed in the United States of America by
BookCrafters, Chelsea, Michigan

87   88   89   90   5   4   3   2   1

Library of Congress Cataloging-in-Publication Data
Jefferson, Thomas, 1743–1826
  Thomas Jefferson's European travel diaries.

  1. Jefferson, Thomas, 1743–1826—Diaries.
2. Jefferson, Thomas, 1743–1826—Journeys—Europe.
3. Europe—Description and travel—17th-18th centuries.
I. Morris, James McGrath.   II. Weene, Persephone.
III. Title.   IV. Title: Travel diaries.
E332.745.J44 1987   914'.04253   87-9991
ISBN 0–9615964–2–2
ISBN 0–9615964–3–0 (pbk.)

Traveling. This makes men wiser but less happy. When men of sober age travel they gather knowledge which they may apply usefully for their country but they are subject ever after to recollections mixed with regret, their affections are weakened by being extended over more objects and they learn new habits which cannot be gratified when they return home.

—Jefferson, August 10, 1787

CONTENTS

INTRODUCTION

by Dean M. Sagar

Thomas Jefferson was forty-three years old when he embarked, in 1787, on the first of his celebrated journeys through the countryside and wine-producing regions of Europe. He had been elected by the Continental Congress nearly three years earlier to serve on a special diplomatic mission in Paris whose purpose was to negotiate as many treaties of friendship and commerce as possible on behalf of the new American republic. Although Jefferson did not anticipate a long stay in France, expecting the mission to last less than two years, it would be five years before he returned to America.

From the distance of the French capital, the author of the Declaration of Independence could only write belated comments to friends on the momentous events in his own country surrounding the drafting and ratification of the U.S. Constitution. But he would witness first-hand the crumbling of the "ancient tyranny" of the French monarchy and remain long enough to influence the adoption of France's Declaration of Rights in August 1789.

Jefferson accepted appointment to Paris as a welcome opportunity to flee the many frustrations of domestic politics and to expand his own education. Two years of controversy and disappointment as governor during 1779–1781, the worst years of the revolution in Virginia, had left him embittered with affairs of state. It was only after the death of his wife, in September 1782, that friends persuaded him to break his solitude and accept election to the Continental Congress. Soon after joining the Congress at Annapolis, however, he became dismayed with the petty squabbles between the delegates of various states and viewed appointment to Paris as a welcome relief and a long-delayed opportunity to observe the societies of Europe.

Jefferson arrived in Paris in August 1784, accompanied by his eldest daughter, Martha. He joined his longtime friends John Adams and Benjamin Franklin, who had remained in France after negotiating the treaty ending the revolutionary war with Britain. The three Americans set to work to revise a 1788 commercial treaty with the French government and to negotiate treaties with Britain, Spain, Portugal and Prussia.

By the spring of 1785, however, they began to view their efforts as futile, having succeeded only in negotiating a political treaty with Prussia. In May an ailing Franklin requested leave to return to America, and Jefferson was appointed his successor as American minister to the French royal court. Adams was sent to a new post in London as minister to Britain. In these posts both men continued to devote themselves to commercial negotiations, with Jefferson concentrating on establishing more equitable trade relations with France. In 1786 Jefferson was still hopeful that needed commercial treaties could be negotiated, and he continued to give major attention to matters of trade and commerce throughout his stay in France.

Jefferson's concern with commerce had little to do with an interest in shipping or the sea and certainly nothing to do with any desire to promote industrial development in America. His primary interest was promoting American agriculture. He thought of his country as largely a nation of farmers, whose richly endowed land would make cultivation of the soil the primary occupation for generations. He regarded commerce as the "handmaid" of agriculture and believed all trade must be free to facilitate the agricultural pursuits of his countrymen. It followed, then, that Jefferson saw his principal duty as American minister to represent agricultural and related commercial interests.

He carefully explained his view of his role to the secretary of foreign affairs, John Jay, in early 1787. "The mass of our countrymen being interested in agriculture, I hope I do not err in supposing that in a time of profound peace as the present, to enable them to adopt their productions to the market, to point out markets for them, and endeavor to obtain favorable terms of reception, is within the line of my duty."

Jefferson's devotion to agriculture reflected more than his concept of duty; it was consistent with his personal interests and basic to his philosophical and political views. He had long believed that agriculture offered the best way of life and the only one that could assure economic and political independence.

As a farmer himself, Jefferson looked to expanded cultivation of a variety of grains and other crops for the promotion of wealth and happiness in his native Virginia. As a theorist, he believed that only men engaged in cultivating the soil were assured of purity, strength and independence. "Those who labor in the earth are the chosen people of God, if ever he had a chosen people," he observed in 1782. "Corruption of morals in the mass of cultivators is a phenomenon of which no age nor nation has furnished an example."

While tolerating commerce as essential to agriculture, Jefferson distrusted other forms of business and large-scale manufacturing, seeing in them the source of corruption in society. And he feared the concentration of workers for the purpose of industry as a source of mischief and political instability. "I consider the classes of artificers [skilled workers] as the panders of vice and instruments by which the liberties of a country are generally overturned," he explained to Jay a year after arriving in France. So strongly did he hold these views that even the prospect of war in late 1786 between Britain and France offered little advantage to America in Jefferson's view. To him it promised only "to do us more injury on the whole by diverting us from agriculture, our wisest pursuit, by turning us to privateering, plunging us into the vortex of speculation, engaging us to over-trade ourselves, and injuring our morals, and in the end our fortunes."

Jefferson's views on the importance of agriculture and trade and the tie between agriculture and human conditions were fully developed before he reached Europe. In his *Notes on Virginia*, which he completed en route to France, he wrote: "While we have land to labor then, let us never wish to see our citizens occupied at a workbench. . . . Let our workshops remain in Europe. . . . The loss by transportation of commodities across the Atlantic will be made up in happiness and permanence of government." Jefferson's observations in Paris and subsequent travels in Europe would do little to change his view that the Industrial Revolution should not be fostered in America and that "steady application to agriculture with just trade enough to take off its superfluities is our wisest course. . . ."

Like his official duties in Paris, Jefferson's European travels reflected his preoccupation with agriculture. The American minister carefully charted his journeys to permit him to inquire first-hand about the trading capacity and products of various seaports, to encourage direct sales of American tobacco, to investigate new strains of rice, wheat and other grains, and to secure samples of olive and fig trees, grapevines and other plants for cultivation in America. During his tour in 1787, he traveled to Hyères on the southern coast to visit an orange grove. He sought out acclaimed olive and fig groves near Nice. And he diverted his journey to cross the Alps and travel as far as Milan in Italy to search for a unique husking machine for Piedmont rice. He even smuggled a sack of rice out of Lombardy, despite the fact there was a penalty of death for anyone caught taking it out of the country. When Jefferson exclaimed "I would go to hell for my country," upon his appointment to Paris in 1784, he clearly intended to do so if it meant securing a new crop or implement for his countrymen. Years later he would consider these acts his most important accomplishments while in France, noting "the greatest service which can be rendered any country is to add a useful plant to its culture."

Jefferson visited farms, orchards and vineyards wherever he traveled, making elaborate notes on equipment, irrigation systems and methods of cultivation and planting. He studied the soil, water and climate for insights into the differences in products and methods that he observed among various regions. He gained his best information from peasants, gardeners and vignerons, deliberately seeking them out as far better informants than the guides, tavern keepers and other "hackneyed rascals" usually encountered by travelers. Jefferson took great pleasure in visiting farms, observing farmers and asking questions. As he explained to his friend the Marquis de Lafayette when halfway through his journey in southern France, "I am never satisfied with rambling through the fields and farms, examining the culture and the cultivators, with a degree of curiosity which makes some take me to be a fool and others to be much wiser than I am."

Jefferson was never too busy noting the soil, crops or climate to observe the conditions of the people living on the lands though which he passed. Consistent with his broad, philosophic view of agriculture, his notes are filled with observations on how people lived, the severity of their labor, their food, their clothing, and the quality of their lives. He was deeply moved by poverty wherever he encountered it. He noted "unequivocal indications of extreme poverty" throughout France and lamented in Germany that the roads from Kleve to Baden were "strung with beggars." Even in the rich lands of Burgundy, he discerned how the varying fortunes of white and red wines were visible in the quality of bread fed to vineyard workers.

He was particularly attentive to the poverty of women, commenting on the drudgery and harshness of the labor of women in Brittany, Turin and Lorraine. He found conditions so deplorable in Béziers as to offer some explanation for women being "driven into whoredom."

Jefferson summarized the approach he employed in observing social conditions when providing advice on travel to Lafayette. "To do it most effectually," he wrote, "you must be absolutely incognito, you must ferret the people out of their hovels as I have done, look into their kettles, eat their bread, loll on their beds under the pretence of resting yourself, but in fact to find if they are soft. You will feel a sublime pleasure in the course of this investigation, and a sublimer one hereafter when you shall be able to apply your knowledge to the softening of their bed or the throwing of a morsel of meat into their kettle of vegetables."

If Jefferson's interest in agriculture dominated his view of his diplomatic duties, his pursuit of agriculture was influenced by his personal interest in wine and viticulture. He experimented with grape growing at Monticello as early as 1770 and continued to inquire about developments in his vineyards while in France. Consistent with his broad views, Jefferson included wine production among the agricultural pursuits in which his countrymen not only could be independent but also commercially successful. In Paris Jefferson had numerous opportunities to sample European wines and to study the vines from which they were made. In October 1785 he noted traveling outside Fontainebleau to meet "the most curious man in France" with regard to plants, who was preparing for him a collection of vines "from which Burgundy, Champagne, Bordeaux, Frontignan and other of the most valuable wines of this country are made." He also noted that another gentleman had collected for him "the best eating grapes."

His position as minister in Paris also encouraged Jefferson to purchase and enjoy the finest European wines he could obtain. From the beginning Jefferson was a generous host and, while junior to both Franklin and Adams, he took upon himself the primary role in entertaining members of the French government. After replacing Franklin as the principal minister in Paris, he interpreted his duties as also involving an almost continuous exercise of hospitality to Americans visiting the city. For Jefferson this was more a pleasure than an obligation; he enjoyed entertaining and sought bright conversation and any news from home. "Mr. Jefferson lives well," Gouverneur Morris reported on a trip to Paris. He "keeps a good table and excellent wines which he distributes freely."

Jefferson was hampered initially by an inability to obtain fine wine in sufficient amounts in Paris at prices he could afford on a minister's salary. Desperate to obtain any wine in quantity by December 1784, he wrote to John Bondfield, the U.S. consul in Bordeaux who had supplied wine for Franklin, requesting that he procure twelve cases of "such wines as he drank at Dr. F's." Jefferson had to wait until April before the cases of Haut Briers [Brion?] arrived. After that he contacted Bondfield at regular intervals requesting large shipments of red Bordeaux and cases of white Grave and Sauterne for his own use and for shipments to friends in America.

Although Jefferson's records indicate that over the years

he favored Bordeaux wines more than those of any other region, his initial use of those wines in Paris was determined in part by their proximity to a seaport that permitted transport to Paris and Jefferson's reliance on Bondfield's judgment on wines and his willingness to cover the costs of shipments until he was reimbursed. Jefferson's records also show purchases of wines from Champagne and both red and white wines from Burgundy. He also expressed a fondness for wines of Frontignan on the southern coast of France, and at least once wrote the U.S. consul in Marseilles in the hope of securing his assistance in obtaining whatever "very good Frontignan as can be obtained." But he had no reliable source of supply for these wines as he had for those of Bordeaux. And even the shipments from Bondfield were often delayed, with several shipments not arriving at all.

It was a mark of Jefferson's increasing knowledge of wine that he soon became impatient with his inability to select the wines that he received and to obtain a broader variety of wines. His correspondence also shows an increasing concern with the quality and authenticity of the wines he did receive. He thus had a personal interest in the itinerary of his agricultural journeys: that of investigating the wines of various regions and establishing "correspondence directly with the owners of the best vineyards" to permit him to request the specific wines he preferred.

While having broader objectives in plotting his journeys in France in 1787 and Germany in 1788, he carefully chose his routes to traverse the principal wine-growing regions. In Paris he purchased maps of the areas, ordered large-scale plans of the cities and the environs, and found guidebooks to some of the places he hoped to visit. He obtained letters of reference to local officials, vineyard owners and wine merchants. For Burgundy he even prepared his own charts showing the villages and the locations of the choice vineyards and added notations of r and w to show where red and white wines were produced. He also arranged for the services of a guide, who would later become his local agent in Burgundy.

Armed with his maps, charts, letters of introduction, guidebooks and personal notebooks, Jefferson left Paris for the south on the last day of February 1787, not to return until

June. It would be the longest continuous journey of his life.

———————

Except for a brief stay in Fontainebleau a year and half earlier, Jefferson had not left the environs of Paris prior to setting out on his southern tour in the spring of 1787. He had planned to return with the French court to Fontainebleau in October 1786 and from there journey south to the seaport cities of the Mediterranean coast. But the American minister's plans were thwarted when he fell and dislocated his wrist. Despite the immediate attention of two physicians, the pain of his injury persisted and he remained confined to his quarters in the Hotel de Langeac for most of the winter. Although able to use his right hand to write letters by December, he noted to friends that his wrist had not become more flexible and that the pain and swelling "remained obstinately the same."

Early in 1787 he revived his plans for a journey south when, having tried every other cure for his wrist, he decided to heed his physicians' advice and try the mineral springs at Aix-en-Provence. A Mediterranean journey also promised relief from the cold and boredom of the Paris winter. True to his southern roots, Jefferson thrived on warmth, and his health and disposition had suffered considerably during each of the winters in Paris.

Jefferson had also become painfully aware of the futility of his social life in the city. As he wrote to a friend in Philadelphia, "I am here burning the candle of life without present pleasure or future object." Believing that "health is the first requisite after morality," Jefferson looked for renewal of both body and spirit in his revived plans for a southern tour.

He set out alone from Paris, following the Seine southeast toward Burgundy. He left his daughter Martha behind to pursue her studies in the prestigious Abbey Royal de Panthémont and shunned both traveling companions and familiar servants. His reason for avoiding the distractions of familiar company was his need of solitude in which to rest and reflect on what he observed. As he explained to an acquaintance after returning to Paris, "I was alone through the whole and think one travels more usefully when alone because he reflects more."

Except when he was aboard the canal boats in Languedoc, Jefferson provided few notes in his journals on how he traveled. Given the speed at which he moved during the early and latter stages of his journey, it can be assumed that he traveled by carriage. He covered one 54-mile segment from outside Paris to Dijon in northern Burgundy in one day. And even though he spent two days in the heart of Burgundy's wine district, he took only eleven days to cover the 250 miles from Sens to Lyon. (He also would have required some form of coach upon leaving Bordeaux to transport to Paris the quantity of wine he appears to have purchased there.) In Italy he had to slow his pace considerably. His letters describe at least one 93-mile segment through the mountains between Nice and Cuneo that he had to travel by mule because the snow was still too heavy to permit more rapid travel.

Whatever his means of transport, Jefferson proved to be a purposeful traveler. It became his habit, one that he would continue the next year in Germany, to walk around the ramparts of a city or town when he arrived and then go to the top of its highest steeple for a bird's-eye view. He would then use the guidebooks and maps he had acquired to identify and locate any sights worth noting. His journals reflect the same purposeful approach to sightseeing, noting only the unusual or noteworthy. He described few conversations, though he must have had many to gather the wealth of information that he did. He permitted himself only occasional comments on his thoughts about or reactions to things or people he encountered and even fewer critical assessments of political conditions in the ill-governed lands of his French hosts. If there is any excess in his notes, it is devoted, like the little time he permitted himself to squander while traveling, to observations made while wandering through farmlands or vineyards, notes on the quality and texture of the soil, the presence or absence of birds, the varieties of plants and flowers, and even the flight of an occasional butterfly.

In the first segment of his journey, from the first of March until he arrived in Aix-en-Provence on March 25, Jefferson traveled the length of the Burgundy region and proceeded southward from Lyon along the Rhône through the vineyards of Côte Rôtie, the Côte du Rhône and Beaujolais until he approached the Mediterranean. He appears to have spent most of his time in Burgundy on the narrow strip of land "about twenty miles long and two miles wide" where the most celebrated wines of the region continue to be produced.

He observed that of the red wines of the region, "Chambertin, Vougeot and Beaune are strongest and will bear transportation and keeping." Among the white Burgundies he clearly preferred the wines of Montrachet and Meursault. He found it "remarkable" that the best of each kind, the Chambertin and Montrachet, were produced at opposite extremes of the region.

From Burgundy he traveled south along the Rhône through canyons so severe that he remarked, "nature never formed a country of more savage appearance than that on both sides of the Rhône." Once again he sought out the region's best wines, finding the best reds at Ampuys and the best whites near Condrieu. He continued on this "river of wine" until Pont Saint-Esprit, where he traveled briefly west to visit Nîmes before turning southeast to Aix-en-Provence. He arrived at the spas of Aix to find the waters a warm 90 degrees Fahrenheit. But after four days of bathing with no apparent benefit to his wrist, he decided to move on to Marseilles, his principal official objective on the Mediterranean coast.

In Marseilles Jefferson appears to have found the solitude he had sought at Aix. He described the city as "an amphitheater surrounded by high mountains of naked rock," and found within it "extensive society, a good theater, freedom from military control and the most animated commerce" of any city on the coast. He spent a week there attending to the official business of inquiring about American shipping and the potential for American trade. But he also made time to visit olive and fig groves, to walk along the shore and ponder the absence of tides on the Mediterranean, and to take excursions to vineyards along the coast. He savored the solitude he found in Marseilles, describing himself in a letter to a friend as "a traveler" who each day "writes, reads, thinks, sleeps just in the moments when nature and the movements of his body and mind require. Charmed with this tranquility, he finds how few are our real wants, how cheap a thing happiness, how expensive a one pride."

Unable to satisfy his curiosity as to "the causes of the difference of the rice of Carolina and that of Piedmont," and hearing of a noteworthy husking machine for rice in Piedmont, he diverged from his intended course for more than a month to cross the Alps into northern Italy. Leaving Marseilles on April 6, he traveled eastward along the French Riviera to Toulon and then across "delicious and extreme plains" to Hyères and Nice. Turning northward, he crossed the mountains toward Turin, and spent his forty-fourth birthday observing the terrain between Scarena and Sospello from the back of a mule. He encountered his first rice fields near Vercelli and found two husking machines before reaching Milan.

Despite his pleasure at being "where Roman taste, genius and magnificence excite ideas" and his desire to see Rome itself, Jefferson reluctantly chose not to proceed beyond Milan. "Milan was the spot at which I turned my back on Rome and Naples," he wrote a friend. "It was a moment of conflict between duty which urged me to return and inclination urging me forward." From Milan he traveled south to Genoa, then returned to France by way of Monaco in early May.

Jefferson's notes during this portion of his journey are surprisingly technical, describing in detail the husking machines he found, the new methods of planting vines he encountered, the process for making Parmesan cheese, and the specifics of a theory he developed, while crossing the mountains, on the hardiness of plants. He ranked them on the basis of their ability to withstand cold. He did not include any comments like those he wrote to close friends on his joy at being "immersed in antiquities from morning to night" or his sense of being "nourished with the remains of Roman grandeur." Nor did he include detailed comments on the wines he found, noting only one, "a red wine of Nebbiolo," that tasted "as sweet as a silky Madeira, as astringent on the palate as Bordeaux, and as brisk as Champagne."

By May 10 Jefferson was back on his original course, moving westward from the Rhône into the royal province of Languedoc. He spent three days in the area between Lunel to Frontignan sampling the sweet muscat wines of the region. His favorites were clearly the white wines of Frontignan. He would place sizeable orders for Frontignan wines from Paris and later from America and would also experiment with growing Frontignan vines at Monticello.

Another principal objective of Jefferson's southern tour was to view the canal of Languedoc to gain information about this "species of navigation" that might assist in developing commerce along Virginia's Potomac river and elsewhere in America. He joined the canal near Béziers and glided along on horse-drawn canal boats for seven days. Because he could only observe at a distance the passing landscape and the "great number of châteaux and good houses in the neighborhood of the canal," he devoted most of his time and notations to observations of the operation of the canal's system of locks and gates. So attentive did he become that at one point he calculated that one-eighth of the time required for navigating the length of the canal was wasted by the operation of an inefficient wooden screw for opening the numerous gates. Jefferson provided these notes to President Washington the next spring, writing that he hoped Washington "may find in them something, perhaps, which may be turned to account... in the prosecution of the Potomac canal."

He continued along the canal until its end at Toulouse, where it joins the Garronne and, beyond that, the Atlantic Ocean. He moved overland along the river until he reached the city of Bordeaux on May 24. He would spend five days in the area surrounding Bordeaux resuming his detailed observations on winemaking. Most of his time was spent in the districts of Médoc and Grave where he noted differences in how vines were planted, grafted and fertilized in each district.

He identified the four vineyards producing red wines "of the finest quality" as being Château Margaux, La Tour de Ségur (Château Latour), Haut-Brion and Lafite, and he chose the 1784 vintage of each of those as being of "superior quality." Seventy years later these vineyards would be awarded *Premier Cru* [first growth] status in the famous classification of Bordeaux wines for the 1855 Paris Exposition. Of the region's white wines he observed that those of Sauterne were "more esteemed in Paris" but those of Grave "most esteemed in Bordeaux."

In the final two weeks of his journey, Jefferson traveled

from Bordeaux to Nantes in Brittany, then along the Loire through Anjou and Touraine to the city of Orleans. He resumed the swift pace of the early part of his journey, and his journal offers only brief comment on the passing countryside. Of the considerable number of vineyards he observed in Anjou, he noted only that many produce "very good wine. . . not equal indeed to the Bordeaux of best quality but to that of good quality and like it." From Orleans he headed north to Paris, arriving on June 12, 1787. Writing to a friend a week later, Jefferson commented that he "never passed three months and a half more delightfully."

Very different circumstances prompted Jefferson to take to the road again in the spring of 1788. Adoption by special convention of a new American constitution and the bitter ratification debates that followed during the winter of 1787–1788 left observers in Europe concerned about the stability of the American government. Jefferson received word in December 1787 that the bankers in Amsterdam who handled American debt payments in Europe would not advance payment to holders of American bonds until the credit of the government could be guaranteed. By March 1788 a sizeable capital debt remained unpaid from January, with a substantial interest payment amounting to 270,000 florins ($356,400) due in June. Jefferson was confronted with negotiating new bonds to cover debt payments or run the risk of default.

The matter become more urgent to Jefferson when he learned that John Adams had received approval for his request to return to America. Not only did he desire to see his close friend before his departure; he thought it imperative to seek Adams's advice on the debt issue, since Adams had been principally involved in negotiating the original debt arrangements. As Jefferson explained to John Jay, Adams's "knowledge of the subject was too valuable to be neglected under the present difficulty." Upon receiving word on March 2 that Adams had formally taken leave of the British court and had already left to attend similar ceremonies at The Hague in the Netherlands, Jefferson made hurried arrangements to join his friend there.

He left Paris on March 4, 1788, on a journey that would last seven weeks. He spent a month of this time in the Netherlands or trying to get there. He was frustrated by delays on his journey to The Hague and, in his increasing anxiety over the possibility of missing Adams, he appears to have taken little pleasure and found little to note about the farmlands he passed. He joined Adams at The Hague, and the two ministers continued together to Amsterdam. They were successful in reaching agreements on the issuance of new bonds to cover payments on their government's outstanding debt, but at the price of having to provide assurance with new bonds for all payments due on American obligations through 1790. The experience did little to enhance Jefferson's view of the "circle of money-lenders" in Amsterdam, and he took little satisfaction in the result of his efforts. As he reported to Jay, "To rescue our credit then, for the present year only, is but to put off the evil day to the next."

Adams soon returned to Britain, leaving Jefferson in Amsterdam to tie up the loose ends of the negotiations. Given this opportunity to tour the city, Jefferson principally noted the mechanical objects that fascinated him. His journal entries at this time are stiff and technical, possibly reflecting his view of the official nature of his presence there, or perhaps the fact that he was bored. His extended stay in the city did afford him an opportunity to make arrangements for his return to Paris and, once again, his thoughts turned mainly to wine. He charted his return trip to take him eastward up the Rhine through the wine-growing regions of Moselle and Rheingau-Rheinhessen and as far southeast as Frankfurt and Heidelberg. He planned to re-enter France at Alsace and travel westward through Lorraine and the vineyards of Champagne on his way to Paris.

Jefferson traveled by carriage, carrying with him maps of all the cities he planned to visit. He joined the Rhine at Utrecht and traveled eastward into Germany. The journal entries he made once underway appear more relaxed and offer general observations of the lands he crossed. He made few comments on agriculture prior to arriving in Cologne and was clearly more outspoken on political matters in Germany than he had permitted himself to be the year before in

France. Perhaps his journal took a somewhat general tone during this segment of his journey because, as he noted when seeking information about an ancient battleground near Duisburg, he found no one "who could understand either English, French, Italian or Latin" to give him the kind of information that had filled his notebooks the year before. But he may also have found little that was unusual in the terrain or culture of the Dutch and German lands he passed. In a letter to his personal secretary he noted that much of what he observed reminded him of upper Maryland and Pennsylvania. "I have been continually amused," he added, "by seeing the origin of whatever is not English among us."

Jefferson renewed his observations on wines while touring vineyards near Cologne. He noted with particular interest that the vineyards were "the most northern spot on earth on which wine is made" but commented only briefly on the origins of the vines and how they are planted. He traveled southward to the vineyards of the Moselle valley, concentrating his attention on the vineyards south of Koblenz where he thought the best Moselle wines were produced. While identifying several Moselles as top quality, he noted that the best, "without any comparison," was made by the Baron Burresheim on the mountain of Brauneberg. It was this wine, in its 1783 vintage, that he would later advise other American travelers to seek if they wished to sample "the best quality of Moselle wine."

It was not until Jefferson reached Frankfurt that his observations on wine and viticulture took on the same level of detail as had his journals of the previous spring. It was in Frankfurt that Jefferson met an old acquaintance, Baron de Geismar, who would become his companion, guide and translator through the vineyards of Rheingau-Rheinhessen. Jefferson had met Geismar nine years earlier, when the German was among the captured British and Hessian officers who, after pledging not to take up arms, were billeted in Charlottesville, near Monticello, while awaiting transport home. Jefferson extended his hospitality to the idled officers and in return acquired considerable knowledge about European conditions and wines.

Accompanied by Geismar, Jefferson visited the vineyards

villages of Johannisberg, Rüdesheim and Hochheim, ling extensive notes on the grape varieties and the ction of the wines. He concluded that it was "from Rüdesheim to Hochheim that wines of the first quality are made" and compiled lists of no less than a dozen properties in each village that produced outstanding wine. Jefferson passed his forty-fifth birthday with Geismar in the vineyards of Hochheim. After returning to Paris he continued to correspond with Geismar, commenting that the Rüdesheim and Hochheim vines they had acquired in the vineyards were thriving in his garden there and pledging that if the German should ever revisit Monticello, "I shall be able to give you there a glass of Hock or Rüdesheim of my own making."

Jefferson's journal provides only brief mention of the vineyards he visited in Alsace. He commented critically that the *vin de paille* made near Colmar, because it is scarce, is "the dearest in the world, without being the best by any means." He resumed his detailed observations of winemaking after entering Champagne near Épernay. Here he noted how the vines were planted and staked, the timing of their harvest, and the different methods of fermentation and bottling for still and sparkling wines. Once again he identified the best producers in the region and commented on the recent vintages. After leaving the vineyards of Champagne, Jefferson passed quickly over the "picturesque" plains between the Seine and the Marne, arriving back in Paris on April 23, 1788.

―――――――

Jefferson's travel diaries offer a unique glimpse not only of life in late eighteenth-century Europe but of a man whose lifelong quest for knowledge and experience has few comparisons in American history. With the possible exception of his friend Benjamin Franklin, no other American displayed so rich a diversity of interests and achievements or played so notable a role in as many fields of human endeavor. The journals reflect the breadth of Jefferson's thinking, his love of observation, and his penchant for detail.

The principal purpose of his journals was to provide a record of the things Jefferson wanted to remember and the information he hoped to use. His journals are not diaries in the aesthetic sense but systematic factual records to be employed for useful purposes. His approach to knowledge was decidedly practical. While he admired intellect that could enlighten or amuse, his was an active, purposeful intellect dedicated to expanding individual freedom and improving social conditions.

The style of the journals is "scientific" as the term was understood in Jefferson's day to apply to the observation of the diverse manifestations of nature. It also implied the disciplined process of analysis and deduction based on observations that Jefferson sought to employ in all his endeavors. He believed "everything in the world is a matter of calculation" and thus within the grasp of human intellect. The key for Jefferson was methodical study and observation of natural phenomena. Given this orientation and the fact that nothing escaped his curiosity, Jefferson became *par excellence* a keeper of records, often collecting the most minute facts to incorporate later in observations or theories that he shared in letters with friends and scholars. In the course of his lifetime he accumulated a treasury of records and documentation of an extent rarely amassed by any individual, let alone by any man as public as Jefferson.

The travel journals are thus part of an extensive body of scientific work produced over the course of Jefferson's lifetime. Although most visible in his only book, *Notes on Virginia*, which he published privately in Paris in 1785, this work fills thousands of pages of the notebooks and journals he kept for fifty years as well as the volumes of his correspondence. What is unique about the travel diaries, however, is the concise, cross-cutting view they provide of the scientific endeavors of a mature Jefferson in a number of important fields of thought and activity. Foremost among these, clearly, is his inquiry into agriculture and viticulture, which permeates every section of the journals and in itself constitutes a formidable body of scholarship.

The journals also offer excellent examples of Jefferson's inquiry into other disciplines, including engineering, mechanics, architecture and invention. Jefferson was, at heart, a builder who considered nothing finished or perfected, whether a piece of equipment, his home at Monticello or human society. His journals are filled with notations on the design or construction of bridges, roads, canals and buildings as well as with the details of every machine or gadget that fascinated him. Two of his own most noted inventions, a folding ladder that he used at Monticello and a moldboard for plows to raise the soil after it had been cut, derived from observations and sketches he made on his journey through Germany in 1788.

But next to agriculture, the area of Jefferson's scientific activity most reflected in the travel journals is natural history. Prior to his southern tour in 1787, Jefferson had gained some reputation as a natural scientist with the publication of the essay on the animal and plant life of North America, that constitutes the largest and most impressive section of his *Notes on Virginia*. Using the data and observations he accumulated in notebooks for twenty years from his readings, his correspondence, his gardens, and his travels in Virginia and other colonies, Jefferson provided impressive documentation of the biological diversity of Virginia and the North American continent. His work challenged many prevailing assumptions of French naturalists and was acclaimed by a fellow scientist in America as "a most excellent natural history. . . possibly equal if not superior to that of any country yet published."

Jefferson's observations of natural phenomena are evident on every page of his travel diaries. He noted in detail the content and texture of the soil wherever he stopped, pronouncing it "reddish," "gravelly," consisting of "mulatto loam," or "stony and indifferent." He gave special attention to trees — commenting to Lafayette while in Italy, "from the first olive fields in Pierrelatte to the oranges of Hyères has been continued rapture to me." He closely observed the conditions under which varieties of trees survived, developing hypotheses in his notes regarding the northern limits in Europe for growing olive trees and an order of various trees "from the tenderest to the hardiest" based on their ability to withstand cold temperatures. Everywhere he commented on the wildlife he observed and, in some instances, the absence of wildlife he had expected — the speckled trout in the rivers of the Piedmont, the cranes near Frankfurt, the absence of rabbits and partridges prior to Lyon, the birds of the Mediterranean coast. He appears to have taken special delight in nightingales wherever he saw or heard them. The journals also offer an example of Jefferson's scientific deduction in the brief discourse seeking to refute a theory advanced by Voltaire and others regarding shells' independent capacity for growth.

Much of Jefferson's contribution to agriculture, botany and natural history centered on his observations and theories relating to the adaptability of plants and animals to temperature. Science involved many activities for Jefferson, among them the study of climate and temperature he conducted daily at Monticello and elsewhere for fifty years. Ironically, he began this effort with the purchase of a thermometer in Philadephia on July 4, 1776, and continued for the rest of his life to make daily observations "as early as possible in the morning and again about 4 o'clock in the afternoon" wherever he happened to be. That he continued this practice during his European tours is evident in the journal notations, made while he paused in Marseilles, summarizing the average morning and afternoon temperatures he had recorded during the eleven days he had been on the Mediterranean coast and noting the longest and shortest days of the year for the region. Clearly, he considered nothing too insignificant to merit his scrutiny.

The importance of Jefferson's springtime journeys in 1787 and 1788 derives from the store of knowledge and information he obtained. His travels and, indeed, his entire stay in Europe, contributed significantly to making Jefferson the most knowledgeable, diverse and interesting American of his generation. His travels were particularly important in providing a broad perspective on European conditions and politics that would prove invaluable in the years following his return to America, not only in his immediate duties as secretary of state, but in his subsequent political and philosophical battles with Alexander Hamilton and his later endeavors as president. Jefferson's political strength was knowledge, not ambition. It was the source of the respect he gained, the authority he held over other men, and the success he achieved.

His tours of Europe's vineyards also contributed significantly to making Jefferson the foremost American authority on wines and viticulture. It provided him, most immediately, with the ability to order the wines he desired, in the vintages he preferred, directly from the producers in Bordeaux and Germany or through trusted agents in Burgundy and the Mediterranean ports. He understood the common terms for discussing selection and shipment of wines, their costs, the best vintage and method for their transportation, and how they should be stored and served. This knowledge, together with his extensive study of grape varieties and their cultivation, brought him recognition as an expert on wines and winemaking whose advice was eagerly sought by friends and strangers alike. His correspondence reveals that he unselfishly shared his knowledge of wines and viticulture with friends, business acquaintances, farmers, scholars and horticulturists and that he served as a wine adviser to four of his fellow presidents, whose terms spanned thirty-six years.

An unexpected result of Jefferson's 1787 travels through the vineyards of France and Italy was his conclusion that cultivation of grapes for wine production should not be promoted in America, at least at that time. The observations he had made regarding the location of Europe's vineyards, the unpredictability of their crops, and the poverty of the vineyard workers led him to conclude that viticulture was not desirable on lands capable of producing other crops and that cultivation of vines was not a desirable occupation in itself.

"We should not wish for their vines," he wrote to a friend two months after his return to Paris. "The culture of the vine is not desirable on lands capable of producing anything else. It is a species of gambling, and of desperate gambling too, wherein whether you make much or nothing, you are equally ruined...accordingly you see much wretchedness among this class of cultivators." He recognized that wine was an agricultural resource for those European countries "whose good soil is otherwise employed" and that had extra people to employ in cultivation. "It is something in the place of nothing," he explained.

But for his country he concluded, grape cultivation "may become a resource to use . . .when the increase of population shall increase our production beyond the demand for them [basic crops] both at home and abroad. Instead of going on to make a useless surplus of them we may employ our supernumerary hands on the vine. But that period has not yet arrived."

Twenty years later, at the close of his term as president, Jefferson would continue to express the view that his countrymen would do best to concentrate on more important agricultural pursuits and rely on trade with Europe to provide wines that were less costly and of higher quality than they could produce. "I have ever observed that my countrymen, who think its introduction important, that a laborer cultivating wheat, rice, tobacco or cotton here will be able with the proceeds to purchase double the quantity of wine he could make," he wrote to an acquaintance in France.

Despite his views on the immediate prospects for an American wine industry, Jefferson never lost confidence that at some future date his country would produce wines that could be commercially successful and equal in quality to the European wines he so admired. Writing in 1808, he predicted, "We could, in the United States, make as great a variety of wines as are made in Europe, not exactly of the same kinds, but doubtless as good." In the technical information he provided scientists and horticulturists, the advice he gave to farmers, and in his own experiments at Monticello, Jefferson would spend the rest of his life striving to make this prophecy a reality.

Arlington, Virginia
February 1987

EDITORS' NOTE

Thomas Jefferson never intended that the travel diaries presented here be published. He kept the diaries as notes to refer to when writing letters and articles about what he saw while traveling in Europe.

Of course, because of the important role Jefferson played in United States history, the diaries have long since made their way into print. They can be found in their entirety in at least two collections of Jefferson's writings and appear abridged in other volumes. As word-for-word transcriptions, those versions are useful for scholars but inaccessible to many general readers.

What we have done in this edition is what Jefferson might have done had he decided to publish his diaries. We've polished the text, making stylistic changes that bring it into line with modern conventions and substantive changes intended to clarify the author's intent.

Changing the spelling was our first task. In most cases it was only a matter of removing a letter that the passage of time has deemed superfluous such as the "h" in "lanthern." In other cases changing the spelling was necessary to prevent misunderstandings. We also brought Jefferson's spelling of place names up-to-date, making it possible for modern travelers to retrace his steps and for wine lovers to taste wines from the vineyards and wineries that he visited.

We revamped his punctuation, taking our lead here from Charles Neider, editor of an excellent edition of Mark Twain's *A Tramp Abroad*. Commenting on that work, Neider said, "The effect of modernizing the punctuation is comparable to that of removing coats of discolored varnish from an old painting."

We converted archaic terms to modern ones. Leagues, for instance, became miles.

We cut out extraneous material that weakened the text and revised portions of the manuscript that might be confusing. That sometimes meant adding words to complete a short-hand sketch or to clarify Jefferson's language. Where incompleteness did not harm readability, however, we did nothing.

Finally, all during the process, we worked with a light hand, striving to keep Jefferson's voice and style intact. We hope the result of our work provides as much pleasure for you, the reader, as it did for us.

—The Editors

THOMAS JEFFERSON'S
EUROPEAN
TRAVEL DIARIES

Words to the Wise from the Author for Americans Traveling Abroad

On arriving in a town, first buy the plan of the place and the book noting its curiosities. Walk around the ramparts when there are any. Go to the top of a steeple to have a view of the town and its environs.

When you are doubting whether a thing is worth the trouble of going to see, recollect that you will never again be so near it and that you may have to repent the not having seen it. But there is an opposite extreme too. That is the seeing of too much. A judicious selection is to be aimed at, taking care that the indolence of the moment has no influence on the decisions.

Take care especially not to let the porters of churches lead you through all the little details in their possession which will load the memory with trifles, fatigue the attention and waste your time. It is difficult to confine these people to the few objects worth seeing and remembering. They wish for your money and suppose you give it more willingly the more detail they provide you.

When one asks in the taverns for the *vin du pays* they give you what is natural and unadulterated and cheap. *Vin étrangère,* on the other hand, is a pretext for charging an extravagant price for an unwholesome stuff, very often of their own brewing.

The people you will naturally see the most of will be tavern keeps, valets and postilions. These are the hackneyed rascals of every country. Of course they must never be considered when we calculate the national character.

Objects Worthy of Attention
for Americans

Agriculture

Everything belonging to this art and whatever is related to it. Useful or agreeable animals that might be transported to America. New species of plants for the farm or garden, according to the climates of the different states.

Mechanical Arts

Things that are necessary in America and cannot be transported ready-made, such as forges, boats and bridges.

Lighter Mechanical Arts

Some of these worth a superficial view. But circumstances rendering it impossible that America should become a manufacturing country during the lifetime of any man now living, it would be a waste of time to examine these minutely.

Gardens

Peculiarly worth the attention of an American because ours is the country of all others where the noblest gardens may be made without expense. We have only to cut out the superabundant plants.

Architecture

Worth the attention of an American because as we double our numbers every twenty years we must double our houses. Besides, we build of such perishable materials that one half of our houses must be rebuilt every twenty years. It is, then, among the most important arts, and it is desirable to introduce taste into an art which shows so much.

Painting, Statues

Too expensive for the state of wealth among us. It would be useless therefore and preposterous for us to endeavor to make ourselves connoisseurs in those arts. They are worth seeing but not studying.

Politics

Well worth studying so far as respects internal affairs. Examine their influence on the happiness of the people. Take every possible occasion of entering into the hovels of the laborers, especially at the moments of repasts. See what they eat, how they are clothed, whether they are obliged to labor too hard, whether the government or their landlords take from them an unjust proportion of their labor, on what footing stands the property they call their own, and their personal liberty.

Courts

To be seen as you would see the Tower of London or Menagerie of Versailles with its lions, tigers and other beasts of prey. A slight acquaintance with these regal assemblies will suffice to show you that under the most imposing exterior they are the weakest and worst part of mankind. Their manners — could you ape them — would not make you beloved in your own country. Nor would they improve America could you introduce them to the exclusion of that honest simplicity now prevailing and worthy of being cherished.

*—Adapted from traveling notes written for
Mr. Rutledge and Mr. Shippen, June 3, 1788.*

Part One

SOUTHERN TOUR
1787

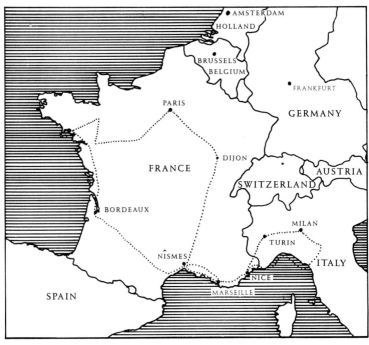

FRANCE

*B*URGUNDY

*At Pommard and Volnay I observed (laborers) eating
good wheat bread; at Meursault, rye. I asked the reason
of this difference. They told me that the white wines
fail in quality much more often than the red and
remain on hand. The farmer therefore cannot afford to
feed his laborer so well. At Meursault only white wines
are made because there is too much stone for the red.
On such slight circumstances depends the condition of man!*

The face of the country, from Sens to Vermonton, is in large hills, not too steep for the plough, somewhat resembling the Elk Hills and Beaverdam Hills of Virginia. The soil is generally a rich, mulatto loam with a mixture of coarse sand and some loose stone. The plains of Yonne are of the same color. The plains are in corn, the hills in vineyards, but the wine is not good. There are a few apple trees but none of any other kind and no enclosures. No cattle, sheep or swine to be seen, but many fine mules.

Few châteaux and no farmhouses, all the people being gathered in villages. Are they thus collected by that dogma of their religion that makes them believe that to keep the Creator in good humor with his own works they must mumble a mass every day? Certain it is that they are less happy and virtuous in villages than they would be insulated with their families on the grounds they cultivate.

The people are badly clothed. Perhaps they have put on their worst clothes at this moment as it is raining. But I observe women and children carrying heavy loads and laboring with the hoe. This is an unequivocal indication of extreme poverty. Men in a civilized country never expose their wives and children to labor above their force and sex, as long as their own labor can protect them from it. I see few beggars, probably the effect of police.

The hills are higher and more abrupt as I approach Dijon. The soil, a good red loam and sand, is mixed with more or less grit, small stone and sometimes rock. All is in corn. Some forest wood here and there, broom, whins [spiny evergreen shrubs] and holly and a few enclosures of quickset hedge. Now and then a flock of sheep can be found.

The people are well clothed, but it is Sunday. They have the appearance of being well fed. Between Maison-neuve and Vitteaux the road leads through an avenue of trees, eight miles long, in a straight line. It is impossible to paint the ennui of this avenue. Crowning the summits of the hills which border the valley in which is Vitteaux there is a parapet of rock, twenty, thirty or forty feet perpendicular. The tops of the hills are nearly level and appear to be covered with earth. Very singular.

In Dijon the tavern price of a bottle of the best wine — for example, wine from Beaune — is four livres. The best round potatoes here I ever saw. They have begun a canal thirty feet wide which will lead into the Saône. It is fed by springs. They are not allowed to take any water out of the river d'Ouche, which runs through this place, on account of the mills on that river. They talk of making a canal to the Seine, the nearest presently navigable part of which is sixty miles from here.

Louis = 20 Livre
Livre = 20 Sous

Eighteenth century currency used in France.

They have very light wagons here for the transportation of their wine. They are long and narrow, and the front wheels are as high as the rear ones. Two *pièces* [casks containing between 130 and 140 gallons] of wine are drawn by one horse in one of the wagons. The road in this part of the country is divided into portions of forty or fifty feet by numbered stones which mark the task of laborers.

Traveling south toward Chagny, I see on the left plains which extend to the Saône, on the right the ridge of mountains called the Côte. The plains are of a reddish-brown, rich loam, mixed with much small stone. The Côte has for its basis a solid rock, on which is about a foot of red soil of middling quality mixed with small stone in equal quantity. The plains are in corn, the Côte in vines. The former have no enclosures; the latter has small ones of dry stone wall. There is a good deal of forest. Some small herds of small cattle and sheep. Fine mules, which come from Provence and cost twenty louis. They break them at two years old and they last to thirty.

The corn lands here rent for about twelve livres the acre. They are now planting, pruning and sticking their vines. When a new vineyard is made they plant the vines in gutters about four feet apart. As the vines advance they lay them down. The vines put out new shoots and fill all the intermediate space until all trace of order is lost. There is ultimately about one square foot to each vine. They begin to yield good profits at five or six years old and last a hundred or a hundred and fifty years.

A vigneron at Volnay carried me into his vineyard, which was of about thirteen acres. He told me that some years it produced him nearly thirty-six hundred gallons of wine and some other years not more than a hundred and eighty gallons. The latter is the most advantageous produce because the wine is better in quality and higher in price in proportion as less is made, and the expenses at the same time diminish in the same proportion. Whereas, when much is made, the expenses are increased, while the price and quality become less.

In very plentiful years they often give away one half the wine for casks to contain the other half. The casks for 250 bottles cost six livres in scarce years and ten in plentiful. The *feuillette* holds 125 bottles, the *pièce*, 250 and the *queue*, or *botte*, 500.

An acre rents at from sixteen to forty-eight livres. A farmer of thirteen acres has about three laborers engaged by the year. He pays four louis to a man and half as much to a woman, and feeds them. He kills one hog and salts it, which is all the meat used in the family during the year. Their ordinary food is bread and vegetables. At Pommard and Volnay I observed them eating good wheat bread; at Meursault, rye. I asked the reason of this difference. They told me that the white wines fail in quality much more often than the red and remain on hand. The farmer therefore cannot afford to feed his laborer so well. At Meursault only white wines are made because there is too much stone for the red. On such slight circumstances depends the condition of man!

The wines which have given such celebrity to Burgundy grow only on the Côte, an extent of about twenty miles long and two miles wide. They begin at Chambertin and go through Vougeot, Vosne, Nuits, Beaune, Pommard, Volnay and Meursault and end at Montrachet. Those of the two last are white; the others, red. Chambertin, Vougeot and Beaune are strongest and will bear transportation and keeping. They sell, therefore, on the spot for 1,200 livres the *queue*, which is forty-eight sous the bottle. Volnay is the best of the other reds, equal in flavor to Chambertin, but being lighter it will not keep and therefore sells for not more than 300 livres the *queue*, which is twelve sous the bottle. It ripens sooner than Chambertin, Vougeot or Beaune do and consequently is better for those who wish to broach at a year old.

In like manner of the white wines and for the same reason, Montrachet sells for 1,200 livres the *queue*, forty-eight sous the bottle, but Meursault of the best quality, such as the Goutte d'Or, at only 150 livres the *queue*, or six sous the bottle. It is remarkable that the best of each kind — that is, of the red and white — is made at the extremities of the line, at Chambertin and Montrachet. It is pretended that the adjoining vineyards produce the same qualities but that belonging to obscure individuals they have not obtained a name and therefore sell as other wines.

The Côte faces a little south of east. The western side is also covered with vines and is apparently of the same soil, yet the wines are of the coarsest kinds. Such, too, are those that are produced in the plains, but there the soil is richer and less strong.

Vougeot is the property of the monks of Cîteaux and produces about twelve thousand gallons of wine. Montrachet contains about sixty acres and produces, one year or another, about seventy-two hundred gallons. It belongs to two proprietors only, Monsieur de Clarmont, who leases to some wine merchants, and the Marquis de Sarsnet, of Dijon, whose part is farmed by a Monsieur de la Tour, whose family for many generations has had the farm.

The best wines are carried to Paris by land. The transportation costs thirty-six livres the *pièce*. The more indifferent go by water.

Again, traveling further south, on the left I see the fine plains of the Saône; on the right, high lands, rather waving than hilly, sometimes sloping gently to the plains, sometimes dropping down in precipices and occasionally broken into beautiful valleys by the streams which run into the Saône. The plains are a dark, rich loam covered with pasture and corn. The heights are more or less red or reddish, always gritty, of middling-quality soil only, their sides in vines and their summits in corn. The vineyards are enclosed with dry stone walls, and there are some quickset hedges in the corn grounds. The cattle are few and indifferent. There are some good oxen, however. They draw by the head.

I passed three times the Canal du Centre, which they are opening from Chalon-sur-Saône to Digoin on the Loire. It passes near Chagny and will be ninety-two miles long. They have worked on it three years and will finish it in four more. It will reanimate the languishing commerce of Champagne and Burgundy by furnishing a water transportation for their wines to Nantes, which also will receive new consequence by becoming the emporium of that commerce. At some distance, on the right, are high mountains, which probably form the separations between the waters of the Saône and the Loire. The people begin now to live in separate establishments and not in villages. Houses are mostly covered with tile.

B_EAUJOLAIS_

*This is the richest country I ever beheld....
They have a method of mixing beautifully the
culture of vines, trees and corn.*

The face of the country is like that from Chalon-sur-Saône to Macôn. The plains are a dark, rich loam, the hills a red loam of middling quality mixed generally with more or less coarse sand and grit and a great deal of small stone. Very little forest. The vineyards are mostly enclosed with dry stone wall. A few small cattle and sheep. Here, as in Burgundy, the cattle are all white.

This is the richest country I ever beheld. It is about forty or forty-eight miles in length and twelve, sixteen or twenty in breadth, at least that part of it which is under the eye of the traveler. It extends from the top of a ridge of mountains, running parallel with the Saône and sloping down to the plains of that river, scarcely anywhere too steep for the plough. The whole thickset with farmhouses, châteaux and the *bastides* [small country houses in southern France] of the inhabitants of Lyons. The people live separately and not in villages.

The hillsides are in vines and corn, the plains in corn and pasture. The lands are farmed either for money or for a portion of the crop. The rents of the corn lands, when they are farmed for money, are about eight or ten livres the acre. A farmer takes perhaps about one hundred twenty acres, for three, six or nine years. The first year they are in corn; the second in other small grain, with which he sows red clover.

The third is for the clover. The spontaneous pasturage is of green sward, which they call *fromenteau*.

When lands are rented for a share of the crop, the cattle, sheep and other animals are furnished by the landlord. A value is set, and they must be left of equal value. The increase of these as well as the produce of the farm is divided equally. These leases are only from year to year.

They have a method of mixing beautifully the culture of vines, trees and corn. Rows of fruit trees are planted about twenty feet apart. Between the trees, in the rows, they plant vines four feet apart and train them on an espalier. The intervals are sowed alternately in corn, so as to be one year in corn, the next in pasture, the third in corn, the fourth in pasture, and so on. Two hundred yards of vines yield generally about two hundred forty gallons of wine. In Dauphine, I am told, they plant vines only at the roots of the trees and let them cover the whole tree. But this spoils both the wine and the fruit. Their wine, when distilled, yields one-third of its quantity in brandy.

The wages of a laboring man here are five louis; of a woman, one half that. The women do not work with the hoe; they only weed the vines and corn and they spin. They speak a patois very difficult to understand.

I passed some time at the Château de Laye Epinaye, where I viewed Monsieur de Laye's *Diana and Endymion*, a very superior morsel of sculpture by Michael Angeloe Slodtz, done in 1740. Monsieur de Laye has a seignory of about twelve thousand acres, in pasture, corn, vines and wood. He has over this, as is usual, a certain jurisdiction both criminal and civil. But this extends only to the first crude examination, which is before his judges. The subject is referred for final examination and decision to the regular judicatures of the country. The seigneur is keeper of the peace on his domains. He is therefore subject to the expense of maintaining it. A criminal prosecuted to sentence and execution costs Monsieur de Laye about five thousand livres. This is so burdensome to the seigneurs that they are slack in criminal prosecutions. A good effect from a bad cause.

Through all Champagne, Burgundy and Beaujolais the husbandry seems good, except that they manure too little.

This proceeds from the shortness of their leases. The people of Burgundy and Beaujolais are well clothed and have the appearance of being well fed. But they experience all the oppressions which result from the nature of the general government and from those of their particular tenures and of the seignorial government to which they are subject. What a cruel reflection, that a rich country cannot long be a free one.

R HÔNE

Nature never formed a country of more savage
appearance than that on both sides of the Rhône...
Yet has the hand of man subdued this savage scene,
by planting corn where there is a little fertility,
trees where there is still less and vines where there is none.

The Rhône makes extensive plains, which lie chiefly on the eastern side and are often in two stages. Those of Montélimar are three or four miles wide and rather good. Sometimes, as in the neighborhood of Vienne, the hills come in precipices to the river, resembling then very much our Susquehanna and its hills, except that the Susquehanna is ten times as wide as the Rhône.

The highlands are often very level. The soil, both of hill and plain, is generally tinged more or less with red. The hills are sometimes mere masses of rock, sometimes a mixture of loose stone and earth. The plains are always stony and as often as otherwise covered so perfectly with a coat of round stones of the size of a fist that they resemble the remains of inundations from which all the soil has been carried away. Sometimes they are middling good, sometimes barren.

In the neighborhood of Lyons there is more corn than wine; toward Tain-L'Hermitage, more vines than corn. From there, the plains, where best, are in corn, clover, almonds, mulberries and walnuts; where there is still some earth, they are in corn, almonds and oaks. The hills are in vines. There is a good deal of forest near Lyons but not much afterwards. Scarcely any enclosures and only a few small sheep before

I reach Tain-L'Hermitage. There the number increases.

Nature never formed a country of more savage appearance than that on both sides of the Rhone. A huge torrent, rushing like an arrow between high precipices, which are often of massive rock, at other times of loose stone with but little earth. Yet has the hand of man subdued this savage scene, by planting corn where there is a little fertility, trees where there is still less and vines where there is none.

On the whole it assumes a romantic, picturesque and pleasing air. The hills on the opposite side of the river, being high, steep, and laid up in terraces, are of a singular appearance. Where the hills are quite in waste, they are covered with broom, whins, box and some clusters of small pines. There were formerly olives at Pains, but a great cold some years ago killed them, and they have not been replanted.

I am told at Montélimar that an almond tree yields about 3 livres of profit a year. Supposing them six yards apart, there will be eighty to the acre, providing 300 livres a year, besides the corn growing on the same ground.

Four miles below Vienne, on the opposite side of the river, is Côte Rôtie. It is a string of broken hills extending four miles on the river, from the village of Ampuis to the town of Condrieu. The soil is white, tinged a little sometimes with yellow, sometimes with red, stony, poor and laid up in terraces. Only those parts of the hills which look to the sun at midday or the earlier hours of the afternoon produce wines of the first quality. Seven hundred vines, three feet apart, yield about one hundred fifty gallons to the acre.

The best red wine is produced at the upper end in the neighborhood of Ampuis; the best white wine, next to Condrieu. They sell the first quality and most recent vintage at 150 livres the *pièce*, equal to twelve sous the bottle. When old, it costs ten or eleven louis the *pièce*. There is a quality that keeps well, bears transportation, and cannot be drunk under four years. Another must be drunk at a year old. They are equal in flavor and price.

The wine called Hermitage is made on the hills impending over the village of Tain-L'Hermitage, on one of which is the hermitage that gives its name both to the hills for about two miles around and to the wine made on them. There are but three of those hills that produce wine of the first quality, and of these the middle regions only are productive. The hills are about three hundred feet in height, three-quarters of a mile in length, and have a southern aspect. The soil is scarcely tinged red, consists of small rotten stone, and is, where the best wine is made, without any perceptible mixture of earth. It is in sloping terraces. They use a little dung.

An *homme de vignes*, which consists of 700 plants three feet apart, yields generally about forty-five gallons of juice. When new, the *pièce* is sold at about two hundred twenty-five livres; when old, at three hundred. It cannot be drunk under four years and improves fastest in a hot situation. There is so little white made in proportion to the red that it is difficult to buy it. They make the white sell the red. If bought separately, it is from fifteen to sixteen louis the *pièce* new and three livres the bottle old. To give quality to the red they mix in one-eighth of white grape. There are but about a thousand *pièces* of both red and white of the first quality made annually.

They leave buds proportioned to the strength of the vine, sometimes as much as fifteen inches. Vineyards are never rented here, nor are laborers in the vineyard hired by the year.

In the neighborhood of Montélimar and below it they plant vines in rows six, eight or ten feet apart and two feet asunder, filling the intervals with corn. Sometimes the vines are in double rows two feet apart. I saw single asses in ploughs proportioned to their strength. The plough is made of three pieces: a beam, to which the ploughshare is attached; a crooked branch of a tree, sometimes forked; and another crooked branch to hold the bar to which the traces of the harness are fastened.

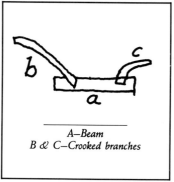

A—Beam
B & C—Crooked branches

tened. Asses or mules, working in pairs, are coupled by square yokes to the rigs.

There are few châteaux in this province. The people are mostly gathered in villages. There is, however, some scattering of farmhouses. These are made either of mud or of round stones and mud. They also make enclosures both those ways.

Day laborers receive sixteen to eighteen sous the day and feed themselves. Men hired by the year receive three louis, women half of that, and both are fed. They rarely eat meat, a single salted hog being the year's stock for a family. But they have plenty of cheese, eggs, potatoes and other vegetables, as well as walnut oil with their salad.

It is a trade here to gather dung along the road for their vines. This proves they have few cattle.

I have seen neither hares nor partridges since I left Paris, nor wild fowl on any of the rivers. The roads from Lyons to Saint-Rambert are neither paved nor graveled. After that they are coated with broken flint. The ferry boats on the Rhône are moved by the stream, and very rapidly. On each side of the river is a movable stage, one end of which is an axle and two wheels that, according to the tide, can be advanced or withdrawn so as to apply to the gunwales of the boat.

The plains on the Rhône here are six or twelve miles wide, reddish, good, and in corn, clover, almonds and olives. Here begins the country of olives, there being very few before this principality of Orange. They are the only tree which I see planted among vines. Thyme grows wild here on the hills.

The remains of the Roman aqueduct here are of brick. A fine piece of mosaic, still on its bed, forms the floor of a cellar. Twenty feet of it is still visible. They are taking down the circular wall of an amphitheatre to pave a road.

*A*RDÈCHE-CÉVENNES

The first butterfly I have seen.

Remoulins has a mixture of hill and dale. From Remoulins to Nîmes I find hills on the right and plains on the left, extending to the Rhône and the sea. The hills are rocky. Where there is soil it is reddish and poor. The plains are generally reddish and good, but stony. When you approach the Rhône, going to Arles, the soil becomes a dark gray loam with some sand and is very good. The culture is corn, clover, sainfoin, olives, vines, mulberries, willows and some almonds. There is no forest. The hills are enclosed in dry stone wall with many sheep. I see many separate farmhouses and a number of people in rags, as well as an abundance of beggars.

The arches of the Pont Saint-Esprit are eighty-eight feet wide. Wild figs, very flourishing, are growing out of the joints of the Pont du Gard.

From the summit of the first hill after the Pont Saint-Esprit there is a beautiful view of the bridge about two miles in the distance and a fine view of the country in both directions. From here an excellent road judiciously conducts the traveler through very romantic scenes. In one part, descending the face of a hill it is laid out serpentine and not ziz-zag to ease the descent. In others it passes though a winding meadow from fifty to a hundred yards wide that is walled on both sides by hills of rock. At length the road comes out into a country of plains.

The waste hills are covered with thyme, box and *chenevert*. Where the body of the mountains has a surface of soil the summit has something of a crown of rock, like that I observed in Champagne.

At Nîmes the earth is full of limestone. And the fountain there is so deep that a stone was thirteen seconds descending from the surface to the bottom.

They are now pruning the olive trees. A very good tree produces sixty pounds of olives, which yields fifteen pounds of oil. The best quality sells for twelve sous the pound retail and ten sous wholesale.

The *vin ordinaire* is good and has a strong body. It costs two or three sous the bottle.

The first butterfly I have seen.

They are nearly finishing at Nîmes a great mill worked by a steam engine which pumps water from a lower into an upper cistern. Water from that cistern is supplied to two overshot wheels [vertical water wheels] that turn two pairs of stones. The water passes through the wheels into the lower cistern and is returned to the upper one by the pumps. A stream of water of one-quarter to one-half inch in diameter replenishes the water lost by evaporation or absorption. This is carried from a well by a horse.

The plains extending from Nîmes to the Rhône in the direction of Arles are broken in one place by a skirt of low hills. They are red and stony at first, but as I approach the Rhone they become a dark gray mold [soil] with a little sand. They are in corn and clover, vines, olives, almonds, mulberries and willows.

At an ancient church in the suburbs of Arles are some hundred ancient stone coffins along the roadside. The ground is called the Champs Elysées. In a vault in the church are some coffins curiously wrought, and in a backyard are many ancient statues and inscriptions.

Within the town are the remains of two Corinthian columns and of the pediment with which they were crowned. It is very ornate, having belonged to the ancient capitol of the place. But the principal monument here is an amphitheatre, the external portico of which is tolerably complete. How many porticos there were cannot be seen, but at one of the principal gates there are still five. They measure, from out to in, 78 feet, 10 inches, the vault diminishing inwards. There are sixty-four arches, each of which is from center to center 20 feet, 6 inches. Of course, the diameter is 438 feet or 450 feet, if we suppose the four principal arches a little larger than the rest.

The ground floor is supported on innumerable vaults. The exterior of the first story has a tall pedestal, like a pilaster, between every two arches. The upper story has a column, the base of which would indicate it to be Corinthian. Every column is truncated as low as the impost [a block on which an arch rests] of the arch. The whole of the inside and nearly the whole of the outside is masked by buildings. It is supposed there are a thousand inhabitants within the amphitheatre. The walls are more entire and firm than those of the amphitheatre at Nîmes. I suspect its plan and distribution to have been very different from that of the latter.

The plains of the Rhône from Arles to Tarascon are four or eight miles wide. From Tarascon to Saint Rémy is another plain, also four or eight miles wide, but bordered by broken hills of massive rock. It is gray and stony and planted mostly in olives. Some almonds, mulberries, willows, vines, corn and lucerne can be seen, as well as many sheep.

A laboring man's wages here are 150 livres, a woman's half, and both are fed. Two hundred eighty pounds of wheat sells for 42 livres. They make no butter here. It costs, when bought, fifteen sous the pound. Oil is ten sous the pound.

Tolerably good olive trees yield, one with another, about twenty pounds of oil. An olive tree must be twenty years old before it has paid its own expense. They last forever. In 1765 it was so cold that the Rhône was frozen over at Arles for two months. In 1767 there was a cold spell of a week that killed all the olive trees. From being fine weather, within one hour there was ice hard enough to bear a horse. It killed people on the road. The old roots of the olive trees put out shoots again later.

Land for olives sells for twenty-four livres the tree and leases at twenty-four sous the tree. The trees are grown fifteen feet apart. However, growing alfalfa is a more profitable trade. An acre yields sixty-three tons of hay a year, worth sixty livres the ton. It is cut four or five times a year. It is sowed broadcast, and the hay lasts five or six years.

An acre of land for corn rents at from thirty-seven to forty-five livres. Leases are for six or nine years. Farmers plant willows for firewood and for hoops for their casks.

There are some châteaux and many separate farmhouses ornamented in a small way so as to show that the tenant's whole time is not occupied in procuring physical necessaries.

After I quit the plains of the Rhône, the country still seems to be a plain, cut into compartments by chains of mountains of massive rock running through it in various directions. The soil is various, gray and clay, gray and stony, red and stony and sometimes barren. I found golden willows.

*P*ROVENCE

The several provinces, and even cantons, are
distinguished by the form of the women's hats,
so that one may know of what canton a woman is by her hat.

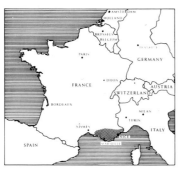

The country is waving in vines and pasture of green sward and clover. Much of it is enclosed with stone, and it is abounding with sheep.

As I approach Aix-en-Provence, the valley, which opens toward the mouth of the Rhône and the sea, is rich and beautiful. A perfect grove of olive trees lines up ahead, among which is corn, alfalfa and vines. The waste ground is rich with thyme and lavender.

Oil of the best quality is twelve sous the pound and sixteen sous if it be virgin oil. This is what runs freely from the olive when it is first put into the press, before pressure is applied. Afterwards the remainder of the oil is forced by the press and by hot water.

Dung costs ten sous the 100 pounds.

The wages of a laboring man are 150 livres the year, a woman's 60 to 65 livres, and both are fed. Their bread — half-wheat, half-rye — is made once in three or four weeks to prevent too great a consumption. In the morning they eat bread with an anchovy or an onion. Their dinner in the middle of the day is bread, soup and vegetables. Their supper is the same. With their vegetables they have always oil and vinegar. The oil costs about eight sous the pound. They drink what is called *piquette*. This is made after the grapes are pressed by pouring hot water on the pomace. On Sunday they have meat and wine.

Their wood for building comes mostly from the Alps,

down the Durance and the Rhône. A log of pine, fifty feet long, girting sixty feet, three inches at one end and three feet, three inches at the other, costs from fifty-four to sixty livres delivered.

Marseilles is in an amphitheatre surrounded by high mountains of naked rock which are eight or twelve miles distant. The country within that amphitheatre is a mixture of small hills, valleys and plains. The latter are naturally rich. The hills and valleys are forced into production. As I look from the Château de Notre Dame de la Garde, it seems as if there is a small country house every few acres.

The country is hilly, intersected by chains of hills and mountains of massive rock. The soil is reddish, stony and indifferent where it is best. Wherever there is any soil, it is covered with olive trees. Among these are corn, vines, some alfalfa, mulberries, some almonds and willows. No enclosures or forest and very few sheep. In the fields open to the sea they are obliged to plant rows of canes every here and there to break the force of the wind. I saw at the Château Borelli pumps worked by the wind. On the road I saw one of those little whirlwinds which we have in Virginia.

Ten morning observations of the thermometer, from the twentieth to the thirty-first of March inclusive, made at Nîmes, Saint Rémy, Aix and Marseilles, give me an average of fifty-two and a half degrees and give forty-six and sixty-one degrees for the least and greatest morning heats. Nine afternoon observations yield an average of sixty and two-thirds degrees and fifty-seven and sixty-six degrees for the least and greatest. They are six or eight months at a time here without rain. Their longest day, from sunrise to sunset, is fifteen hours and fourteen minutes; the shortest is eight hours and forty-six minutes.

There are no tides in the Mediterranean. It is observed to me that the olive tree grows nowhere further than 120 miles away from that sea. I suppose, however, that both Spain and Portugal furnish proofs to the contrary and doubt the observation's truth as to Asia, Africa and America.

The most delicate figs known in Europe are those growing about this place, called *figues Marcelloises*, or *les veritables Marcelloises*, to distinguish them from others of inferior quality growing here. These keep any length of time. All others exude a sugar in the spring of the year and become sour. The only process for preserving them is drying them in the sun without putting anything to them whatever. They sell at fifteen sous the pound, while there are others as cheap as five sous the pound.

Pretty good fig trees are about the size of an apricot tree, and each yields about twenty pounds of dry figs. The trees are sometimes fifteen inches in diameter. It is said the Marseilles fig degenerates when transported into any other part of the country.

I found here a small dried grape from Smyrna, Turkey, without a seed. There are a few plants growing in this neighborhood. The best grape for drying known here is called *des panses*. They are very large, with a thick skin and much juice. They are best against a wall of southern aspect as the abundance of juice requires a great deal of sun to dry it.

The caper is a creeping plant. It is killed to the roots every winter. In the spring it puts out branches, which creep to the distance of three feet from the center. The fruit forms on the stem as that extends itself and must be gathered every day as it forms. This is the work of women. It is pickled and used for seasoning. The pistachio grows in this neighborhood also but is not very good. They eat them in their milky state.

Monsieur de Bergasse has a wine cellar 240 feet long in which are 120 casks of 10,000 to 13,000 gallons each. These casks are 12 feet in diameter; the staves are four inches thick and the heading two and a half inches thick. The temperature of his cellar is seventy-two degrees. The best method of packing wine when bottled, I'm told, is to lay the bottles on their side and cover them with sand.

Traveled from Marseilles to Aubagne by a valley bordered on each side by high mountains of massive rock on which are only some small pines. The interjacent country is of small hills, valleys and plains. Those are reddish, gravelly and originally poor, but fertilized by art and covered with corn, vines, olives, figs, almonds, mulberries, lucerne and clover. The river Huveaune is twelve or fifteen feet wide, one or two feet deep, and rapid.

From Aubagne to Le Beausset and Toulon I followed a road that quit the wealthy valley a little after Aubagne and entered those mountains of rock for about a dozen miles. Then it passed six or eight miles through a country still very hilly and stony but laid up in terraces and covered with olives, vines and corn. It then followed for two or three miles a hollow between two of those high mountains which has been found or made by a small stream. The mountains, then reclining a little from their perpendicular and presenting a coat of soil, reddish and tolerably good, gave place to the little village of Ollioules, in the gardens of which are oranges in the open ground.

The road remained hilly until I entered the plain of Toulon. On different parts of this road there are figs in the open fields. At Cuers is a plain of about three-fourths of a mile in diameter, surrounded by high mountains of rock. In this the caper is principally cultivated. The soil is mulatto, gravelly and of middling quality, or rather indifferent. The plants are set one at each corner of a square and one at the center and are covered during winter with a hill of earth a foot high. They are now enclosing, pruning and ploughing them.

From Ollioules to Toulon the figs are in the open fields. Some of them have stems of fifteen inches' diameter. They generally fork near the ground, but sometimes have a single stem five feet long. They are as large as apricot trees. The olive trees of this day's journey are about the size of large apple trees.

Toulon is in a valley at the mouth of the Goutier, a little river of the size of the Huveaune, surrounded by high mountains of naked rock that leave some space between them and the sea. This ground is hilly, reddish, gravelly and of middling quality, in olives, vines, corn, almonds, figs and capers.

The capers are planted eight feet apart. A bush yields, one year with another, two pounds, worth twelve sous the pound. Every plant, then, yields twenty-four sous, equal to one shilling sterling. An acre containing 676 plants would yield thirty-three pounds, sixteen shillings sterling. The fruit is gathered by women, who can take about twelve pounds a day. These plants grow equally well in the best or worst soil, or even in the walls where there is no soil. They will last longer than the life of a man. Where the caper is in a soil that will admit ploughing, they do so.

The heat is so great at Toulon in summer as to occasion very great cracks in the earth. They have peas here through the winter, sheltering them occasionally.

Hyères is a plain two or three miles across, bounded by the sea on one side and mountains of rock on the other. The soil is reddish, gravelly, tolerably good and well watered. It is in olives, mulberries, vines, figs, corn and some flax. There are also some cherry trees. From Hyères to the sea, which is two or three miles, is a grove of orange trees, olives and mulberries. The largest orange tree is two feet in diameter one way and one foot the other — for all the trunks of the larger ones are oval, not round — and about twenty feet high. Such a tree will yield about sixty-six hundred oranges a year. The cold of the last November killed the leaves of a great number of the orange trees and some of the trees themselves.

The garden of Monsieur Fille has 15,600 orange trees. Some years they yield 40,000 livres, some only 10,000, but generally about 25,000. The trees are from eight to ten feet apart. They are blossoming and bearing all the year, flowers and fruit in every stage at the same time. But the best fruit is that which is gathered in April and May.

Hyères is a village of about five thousand inhabitants, at the foot of a mountain which covers it from the north and from which extends a plain of two or three miles to the seashore. It has no port. Here are palm trees twenty or thirty feet high, but they bear no fruit. There is also a botanical garden kept by the king. Considerable salt ponds here.

Hyères is six miles from the public road. It is built on a narrow spur of the mountain. The streets in every direction are steep, in steps of stairs, and about eight feet wide. No carriage of any kind can enter it. The wealthiest inhabitants use *chaises a porteurs*. But there are few wealthy, the bulk of the inhabitants being laborers of the earth. Four miles out in the sea is an island on which is the Château de Giens, belonging to the Marquis de Pontoives. There is a causeway leading to it.

From Hyères to Cuers and le Luc is mostly a plain, with mountains on each hand at a distance of a mile or two. The soil is generally reddish, and the latter part is very red and good. The growth is olives, figs, vines, mulberries, corn, clover and alfalfa. The olive trees are from three to four feet in diameter. There are hedges of pomegranates, sweetbriar and broom. A great deal of thyme growing wild. There are some enclosures of stone for sheep and goats.

The road from le Luc to Vidauban, Muy and Frejus leads through valleys and crosses occasionally the mountains which separate them. The valleys are tolerably good, always red and stony, gravelly or gritty. Their produce is as in others before. The mountains are barren.

Eighteen miles of ascent and descent of a very high mountain take me from Esterelle to la Napoule. From there the road is generally near the sea, passing over little hills or strings of valleys, the soil stony and much below mediocrity in its quality. Here and there is a good plain.

There is snow on the high mountains. The first frogs I have heard are of this day, the ninth of April. At Antibes are oranges in the open ground, but in small enclosures; palm trees also. From here to Var are the largest fig trees I have seen. The trees are eighteen inches in diameter and six feet in height to the stem. The olive trees are sometimes six feet in diameter, with heads as large as those of the largest dwarf apple trees. This tree was but a shrub where I first fell in with it and has become larger and larger to this place.

The people are mostly in villages. The several provinces, and even cantons, are distinguished by the form of the women's hats, so that one may know of what canton a woman is by her hat.

With respect to the orange, there seems to be no climate on this side of the Alps sufficiently mild in itself to preserve it without shelter. At Ollioules, they are between two high mountains; at Hyères, covered on the north by a very high mountain; at Antibes and Nice, covered by mountains and also within small high enclosures. A topic for future inquiry: to trace the true line from east to west which forms the northern and natural limit of that fruit.

Saw an elder tree *(sambucus)* near Nice, fifteen inches in diameter, and an eight foot stem. The wine made in this neighborhood is good, though not of the first quality. There are 1,000 mules, loaded with merchandise, which pass every week between Nice and Turin, counting those coming as well as going.

There are no orange trees after the environs of Nice. I lose the olive after rising a little above the village of Scarena, on Mount Braus, and find it again on the other side, a little before getting down to Sospel. But wherever there is soil enough, it is terraced and in corn. The waste parts are either in two-leaved pine and thyme or of absolutely naked rock. Sospel is on a little torrent, called Bevera, which runs into the river Roia, at the mouth of which is Ventimiglia. The olive trees on the mountain are now loaded with fruit, while some at Sospel are in blossom.

In crossing Mount Brois, I lose the olive tree after getting to a certain height, and I find it again on the other side at the village of Breglio. Here I come to the river Roia, which, after receiving the branch on which is Sospel, leads to the sea. The Roia is about twelve yards wide, and it abounds with speckled trout. Were a road made from Breglio along the side of the Roia to Ventimiglia, it might turn the commerce of Turin to that place instead of to Nice because it would avoid the mountains of Braus and Brois, leaving only that of Tende. That is to say, it would avoid more than half the difficulties of the passage.

Further on, as I come to the Château di Saorgio, a scene is presented that is the most singular and picturesque I ever saw. The castle and village seem hanging to a cloud in front. On the right is a mountain through whose split passes a gurgling stream. On the left, a river, over which is thrown a magnificent bridge. The whole forms a basin, the sides of which are shagged with rocks, olive trees and vines.

Near here I saw a tub wheel without a ream. The trunk descended from the top of the waterfall to the wheel, in a direct line, but with the usual inclination. The produce along this passage is most generally olives, except on the heights where it is as before observed; also there are corn, vines, mulberries, figs, cherries and walnuts. They have cows, goats and sheep. As I pass on towards Tende, olives fail ultimately at the village of Fontan, and there the chestnut trees begin in good quantity. Ciandola consists of only two houses, both taverns. Tende is a very inconsiderable village, in which they have yet to know the luxury of a glass window. Nor in any of the villages on this passage have they yet the fashion of powdering the hair. Common stone and limestone are so abundant that the apartments of every story are vaulted with stone, to save wood.

ITALY

*P*IEDMONT

*There is a red wine of Nebbiolo made in the
neighborhood which is very singular. It is about
as sweet as the silky Madeira, as astringent on
the palate as Bordeaux and as brisk as Champagne.*

From Limone I see an abundance of limestone where the earth is not covered with snows, from within half or three-quarters of an hour's walk of the top to the foot of the mountain. The snows descend much lower on the eastern than the western side. Wherever there is soil there is corn, right up to the commencement of the snows and, I suppose, under them also. The waste parts are in two-leaved pine, lavender and thyme.

From the foot of the mountain to Cuneo, the road follows a branch of the Po, the plains of which begin narrow and widen at length into a general plain country, bounded on one side by the Alps. They are good, dark-colored, sometimes tinged with red and in pasture, corn, mulberries and some almonds. The hillsides bordering these plains are reddish and where they admit of it are in corn, but this is seldom. They are mostly in chestnuts and often absolutely barren.

The whole of the plains is plentifully watered from the river, as is much of the hillside. A great deal of golden willow all along the rivers on the whole of this passage through the Alps. The southern parts of France, but still more the passage through the Alps, enable one to form a scale of the tenderer plants, arranging them according to their several powers of resisting cold. Ascending three different mountains, Braus, Brois and Tende, they disappear one after another, and descending on the other side they show themselves again one after another. This is their order, from the tenderest to the hardiest: caper, orange, palm, aloe, olive, pomegranate, walnut, fig and almond. But this is only in regard to the plant, for as to the fruit the order is somewhat different. The caper, for example, is the tenderest plant, yet being so easily protected it is the most certain in its fruit. The almond, the hardiest plant, loses its fruit in these parts. Cuneo is a considerable town and pretty well built. It is walled.

The Alps, as far as they are in view from north to south, show the gradation of climate by the line which terminates the snows lying on them. This line begins at their foot northwardly and rises as they pass on to the south so as to be halfway up their sides on the most southern undulations of the mountain now in view. From the mountains to Turin I see no tree tenderer than the walnut. Of these, as well as of almonds and mulberries, there are a few. Somewhat more in vines, but most generally willows and poplars. Corn is sowed with all these. They mix with them also clover and small grasses.

The country is generally plains, the soil dark and sometimes, though rarely, reddish. It is rich and much infested with wild onions. At Racconigi I see the tops and shocks of corn, which proves it is cultivated here. But it can be in small quantities only because I observe very litle ground but that already has something else in it. Here and there are small patches prepared, I suppose, for corn.

They have a method of planting vines which I have not seen before. At intervals of about eight feet they plant from two to six vines in a cluster. At each cluster they fix a forked staff. The plane of the prongs of the fork is at a right angle with the rows of vines. Across these prongs they lash another staff, like a handspike, about eight feet long horizontally, seven or eight feet from the ground. Of course, it crosses the rows at right angles. The vines are brought from the foot of the fork up to this crosspiece, turned over it, and conducted along over the next, and so on as far as they will extend. The whole forms an arbor eight feet wide and high and of the whole length of the row, little interrupted by the stems of the vines, which — being close around the fork — pass up through hoops, so as to occupy little space.

All the buildings in this country are of brick, sometimes covered with plaster, sometimes not. There is a very large and handsome bridge of seven arches over the torrent of Sangone. I cross the Po in swinging boats. The boats are placed side by side and kept together by a plank floor common to both and lying on the gunwales. The carriage drives on this, without any of the horses being taken out.

About one hundred and fifty yards up the river is a fixed stake and a rope tied to it, the other end of which is made fast to one side of the boats so as to throw them oblique to the current. The stream then acting on them, as on an inclined plane, forces them cross the current in the portion of a circle of which the rope is the radius. To support the rope in its whole length there are two intermediate canoes about fifty yards apart, in the heads of which are short masts. To the top of these the rope is lashed, the canoes being free otherwise to concur with the general vibration in their smaller arcs of circles. The Po is about fifty yards wide there and about a hundred yards in the neighborhood of Turin.

I observe here workers carrying very long beams of wood on two pairs of wheels, which the beam connects together.

The first nightingale I have heard this year; it is today April eighteenth. There is a red wine of Nebbiolo made in the neighborhood, which is very singular. It is about as

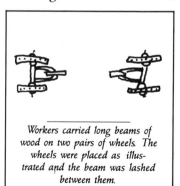

Workers carried long beams of wood on two pairs of wheels. The wheels were placed as illustrated and the beam was lashed between them.

sweet as the silky Madeira, as astringent on the palate as Bordeaux and as brisk as Champagne. It is a pleasing wine.

At Moncalieri, about six miles from Turin, on the right

side of the Po begins a ridge of mountains, which, following the Po near Turin, after some distance spreads wide and forms the duchy of Montferrato. The soil is mostly red and in vines, affording a wine called Montferrato which is thick and strong.

The country continues as a rich plain, its soil black. The culture consists of corn, pasture, maize, vines, mulberries, walnuts and some willows and poplars. There is little maize in proportion to the smaller grains. The earth is formed into ridges from three to four feet wide and the maize sowed broadcast on the higher parts of the ridge so as to cover a third or a half of the whole surface. It is sowed late in May.

This country is plentifully and beautifully watered at present. Much is done by torrents which are dry in summer. The torrents make a great deal of waste ground, covering it with sand and stones. These wastes are sometimes planted in trees, sometimes quite unemployed. They make hedges of willows by setting the plants from one to three feet apart. When they are grown to the height of eight or ten feet, the people bend them down and interlace them one with another. I do not see any of these, however, which are become old — probably they soon die.

Willows are interlaced to form hedges.

The women here smite on the anvil and work with the maul and spade. The people of this country are ill-dressed in comparison with those of France, and there are more spots of uncultivated ground. They use goads for the oxen, not whips. The first swallows I have seen are today.

There is a wine called Gattinara, made in the neighborhood of Vercelli, in both red and white. The latter resembles Calcavallo. There is also red wine of Salusola which is esteemed. It is very light.

In the neighborhood of Vercelli begin the rice fields. The water which these use is very dear. They do not permit rice to be sown within two miles of the cities on account of the insalubrity. Notwithstanding this, when the water is drawn off the fields in August, the whole country is subject to agues [malarial fever] and fevers. They estimate that the same measure of ground yields three times as much rice as wheat and with half the labor. They are now sowing. As soon as the fields are sowed, they let on the water two or three inches deep. After six weeks or two months, they draw it off to weed, then let it on again, and it remains till August, when it is drawn off — about three or four weeks before the grain is ripe. In September they cut the grain.

It is first threshed, then beaten in a mortar to separate the husk; then, by different siftings, it is separated into three quantities. Twelve *rupes*, equal to 300 pounds of twelve ounces each, sell for sixteen livres, money of Piedmont, where the livre is exactly the shilling of England.

The machine for separating the husk is made in the following manner. In the axis of a water wheel a number of arms are inserted which, as they revolve, catch each the cog of a pestle, lift it to a certain height, and let it fall again. These pestles are five and a quarter inches square, ten feet long, and at their lower end formed into a truncated cone of three inches in diameter where cut off. The conical part is covered with iron. The pestles are ten and a half inches apart in the clear. They pass through two horizontal beams, which string them together, and while the mortises [holes or grooves] in the beams are so loose as to let the pestles work vertically, they restrain them to that motion. There is a mortar of wood twelve or fifteen inches deep under each pestle, covered with a board, the hole of which is only large enough to let the pestle pass freely. There are two arms in the axis for every pestle, so the pestle gives two strokes for every revolution of the wheel.

Poggio, a muleteer who passes every week between Vercelli and Genoa, will smuggle a sack of rough rice for me to Genoa; it is death to export it in that form.

From Vercelli to Novara the fields are all in rice and now mostly under water. The dams separating the several ponds are set in willows. At Novara there are some figs in the gardens, in situations well protected. From Novara to Ticino it is mostly stony and waste, grown up in broom. From Ticino to Milan it is all in corn. Among the corn are willows, a good many mulberries, some walnuts and here and there an almond. The country still a plain, the soil black and rich, except between Novara and the Ticino, as before mentioned. There is very fine pasture round Vercelli and Novara to the distance of two miles, within which rice is not permitted.

I cross the Sisto on the same kind of vibrating or pendulum boat as on the Po. The river is eighty or ninety yards wide; the rope fastened to an island two hundred yards above and supported by five intermediate canoes. It is about one and a half inches in diameter. On these rivers they use a short oar of twelve feet long, the flat end of which is hooped with iron, shooting out a prong at each corner, so that it may be used occasionally as a setting pole.

They have still another method here of planting the vine. Along rows of trees they lash poles from tree to tree. Between the trees are set vines, which, passing over the pole, are carried on to the pole of the next tree, whose vines are in like manner brought to this and twined together, thus forming the intervals between the rows of trees alternately into arbors and open space. They have another method also of making quickset hedges. Willows are planted from one to two feet apart and interlaced so that every one is crossed by three or four others.

Figs and pomegranates grow here in Milan unsheltered, I am told. I saw none and therefore suppose them rare. They had formerly olives, but a great cold in 1709 killed them, and they have not been replanted. Among a great many houses painted *al fresco*, the Casa Roma and Casa Candiani, by Appiani, and the Casa Belgioioso, by Martin, are superior. In the second is a small cabinet, the ceiling of which is in small hexagons within which are cameos and heads painted alternately, no two the same. The salon of the Casa Belgioioso is superior to anything I have ever seen. The mixture called *scagliola*, of which they make their walls and floors, is so like the finest marble as to be scarcely distinguishable from it.

On two nights while I was here the rice ponds froze half an inch thick. Droughts lasting two or three months are not uncommon here in summer. About five years ago there was such a hail as to kill cats.

The Count del Verme tells me of a pendulum odometer for the wheel of a carriage.

At Cassio, five miles from Milan, I examined another rice-beater of six pestles. They are eight feet, nine inches long. Their ends, instead of being truncated cones, have nine teeth of iron bound closely together. Each tooth is a double pyramid joined at the base. When put together, they stand with the upper ends placed in contact, so as to form them into one great cone, with the lower ends diverging. The upper are

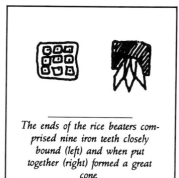

The ends of the rice beaters comprised nine iron teeth closely bound (left) and when put together (right) formed a great cone.

socketed into the end of the pestle, and the lower, when a little blunted by use, are not unlike the jaw teeth of a mammoth, with their studs. They say here that pestles armed with these teeth clean the rice faster and break it less. The mortar is of stone, which is supposed as good as wood and more durable. One half of these pestles are always up. They rise about twenty-one inches, and each makes thirty-eight strokes in a minute.

One hundred pounds of rough rice is put into the six mortars and beaten somewhat less than a quarter of an hour. It is then taken out, put into a sifter of four feet in diameter that is suspended horizontally; sifted there; shifted into another of the same size; sifted there; returned to the mortars; beaten a little more than a quarter of an hour; sifted again; and it is finished. The six pestles will clear 4,000 pounds in twenty-four hours. The pound here is twenty-eight ounces, the ounce being equal to that of Paris. The best rice requires half an hour's boiling; a more indifferent kind, somewhat less.

To sow the rice, they first plough the ground, then level it with a drag harrow and let on the water. When the earth has become soft, they smooth it with a shovel under the water and then sow the rice in the water.

It is supposed that Parmesan cheese was formerly made at Parma and took its name thence, but none is made there now. It is made through all the country extending from Milan for 150 miles. The most is made about Lodi.

Because the making of butter is connected with that of making cheese, both must be described together. There are, in the stables I saw, eighty-five cows fed on hay and grass, not on grain. They are milked twice in twenty-four hours, ten cows yielding at the two milkings a *brenta* of milk, which is twenty-four of our gallons. The night's milk is skimmed in the morning at daybreak, when the cows are milked again and the new milk mixed with the old. In three hours the whole mass is skimmed a second time, the milk remaining in a kettle for cheese and the cream being put into a cylindrical churn, shaped like a grindstone, with a radius of eighteen inches and a thickness of fourteen inches.

In this churn there are three staves pointing inward, endwise, to break the current of the milk. Through its center passes an iron axis with a handle at each end. It is turned about an hour and a half by two men till the butter is produced. Then they pour off the buttermilk and put in some water which they agitate backwards and forwards about a minute and then pour off. They take out the butter, press it with their hands into loaves and stamp it. It has no other washing. Sixteen American gallons of milk yield fifteen pounds of butter, which sell at twenty-four sous the pound.

The milk, which after being skimmed as before has been put into a copper kettle, receives its due quantity of rennet and is gently warmed if the season requires it. In about four hours the whey begins to separate. A little of it is taken out. The curd is then thoroughly broken by a machine like a chocolate mill. A quarter of an ounce of saffron is put to seven *brenta* of milk to give color to the cheese.

The kettle is then moved over the hearth and heated by a quick fire till the curd is hard enough to be broken into small lumps by continued stirring. It is moved off the fire, most of the whey taken out, the curd compressed into a globe by hand, and a linen cloth slipped under it in which it is drawn out. A loose hoop is then laid on a bench and the curd, wrapped in the linen, is put into the hoop. After the curd is pressed a little by hand, the hoop is drawn tight and made fast. A board two inches thick is laid on it, then a stone of about twenty pounds weight. In an hour the whey is run off and the cheese finished.

They sprinkle a little salt on it every other day in summer and every day in winter, for six weeks. Seven *brentas* of milk make a cheese of 50 pounds, which requires six months to ripen and is then dried to 45 pounds. It sells on the spot for eighty-eight livres the 100 pounds. There are now 150 cheeses in this dairy. They are nineteen inches in diameter and six inches thick. They make a cheese a day in summer and two in three days or one in two days in winter.

The whey is put back into the kettle, the buttermilk poured into it, and of this they make a poor cheese for the country people. Another cheese, *mascarponi*, a kind of curd, is made by pouring some buttermilk into cream, which is thereby curdled and is then pressed into a linen cloth. The whey of this is given to the hogs. Eight men suffice to keep the cows and to do all the business of this dairy.

The icehouses at Rozzano are dug about fifteen feet deep and twenty feet in diameter, and poles are driven down all round. A conical thatched roof is then put over them, about fifteen feet high, and pieces of wood are laid at the bottom to keep the ice out of the water, which drips from it and goes off by a sink. Straw is laid on this wood and then the house filled with ice, always with straw between the ice and the walls and the ice covered ultimately with straw. About a third is lost by melting. Snow gives the more delicate flavor to creams, but ice is the more powerful congealer and lasts longer. A tuft of trees surrounds these icehouses.

Around Milan, at a distance of five miles, are corn, pastures, gardens, mulberries, willows and vines. For in this state rice ponds are not permitted within five miles of the cities.

Near Cassio the rice ponds begin and continue to within five miles of Pavia, the whole ground being in rice, pasture and willows. The pasture is in the rice grounds which are resting. In the neighborhood of Pavia again are corn and pasture, as around Milan. They gave me green peas at Pavia.

LIGURIA

If any person wished to retire from his acquaintance to live absolutely unknown and yet in the midst of physical enjoyments, it should be in some of the little villages of this coast, where air, water and earth concur to offer what each has most precious.

From Pavia to Novi, corn, pasture, vines, mulberries, willows, but no rice. The country continues in plains, except that the Appenines are approaching on the left. The soil, always good, is dark till I approach Novi and then is red. I cross the Po where it is 300 yards wide in a pendulum boat. The rope is fastened on one side of the river, 300 yards above it, and supported by eight intermediate canoes with little masts in them to give a greater elevation to the rope. I pass in eleven minutes. Women, girls and boys are working with the hoe and breaking the clods with mauls.

At Novi the Appenines begin to rise. Their growth of timber is oak, tall, small and knotty, and chestnut. With the ascent, walnuts soon vanish, to appear again about one-fourth of the way down on the south side. About halfway down I find figs and vines, which continue fine and in great abundance. The Appenines are mostly covered with soil and are in corn, pasture, mulberries and figs, in the parts before indicated. About halfway from their foot to Genoa, at Campo-Marone, I find again the olive tree. Hence the produce becomes mixed of all the kinds mentioned before.

The method of sowing the Indian corn at Campo-Marone

is as follows. With a hoe shaped like the blade of a trowel, two feet long and six inches broad at its upper end, pointed below and a little curved, they make a trench. In that they drop the grains six inches apart. Then, two feet away they make another trench, throwing the earth that they take out of that on the grain of the last one with a singular skill and quickness, and so through the whole piece. The last trench is filled with the earth adjoining.

Scaffold poles are used for the upper parts of a wall in Genoa, for the third story. They rest on the window sills of the story below. Slate is used here for paving, for steps, for stairs — the rise as well as tread — and for fixed Venetian blinds. At the Palazzo Marcello Durazzo there are benches with straight legs and bottoms of cane.

At Nervi they have peas and strawberries all the year round. The gardens of the Count Durazzo at Nervi exhibit as rich a mixture of *utile dulci* [the useful with the pleasant] as I ever saw. All the environs of Genoa are in olives, figs, oranges, mulberries, corn and garden stuff.

From Noli the Apennines and the Alps appear to me to be one and the same continued ridge of mountains separating everywhere the waters of the Adriatic Gulf from those of the Mediterranean. Where it forms an elbow — touching the Mediterranean as a smaller circle touches a larger within which it is inscribed in the manner of a tangent — the name changes from Alps to Apennines.

It is the beginning of the Apennines which constitutes the state of Genoa, the mountains there generally falling down in barren, naked precipices into the sea. Wherever there is soil on the lower parts, it is principally in olives and figs or in vines, mulberries and corn. Where there are hollows well protected, there are oranges.

Noli, into which I was obliged to put by a change of wind, is forty miles from Genoa. There are 1,200 inhabitants in the village and many separate houses round about. One of the precipices hanging over the sea is covered with aloes. But neither here nor anywhere else I have been could I procure satisfactory information that they ever flower. The current of testimony is to the contrary.

Paths penetrate up into the mountains in several directions about three-fourths of a mile, but these are practicable only for asses and mules. I saw no cattle or sheep in the settlement. The wine they make is white and indifferent.

An oil and vinegar cruet seen in Italy

I heard a nightingale here.

In walking along the shore from Louano to Albenga, I saw no appearance of shells. The tops of the mountains are covered with snow, while there are olive trees on the lower parts.

I do not remember having been told the cause of the apparent color of the Mediterranean. Its water is generally clear and colorless if taken up and viewed in a glass. Yet in the mass it assumes by reflection the color of the sky or the atmosphere, becoming black, green or blue according to the state of the weather.

If any person wished to retire from his acquaintance to live absolutely unknown and yet in the midst of physical enjoyments, it should be in some of the little villages of this coast, where air, water and earth concur to offer what each has most precious. Here are nightingales, beccaficos, ortolans, pheasants, partridges, quails, a superb climate and the power of changing it from summer to winter at any moment by ascending the mountains. The earth furnishes wine, oil, figs, oranges and every production of the garden in every season. The sea yields lobsters, crabs, oysters, tunny, sardines and anchovies.

Through the whole of my route from Marseilles I observe they plant a great deal of cane or reed, which is convenient while growing as a cover from the cold and boisterous winds and, when cut, serves for espaliers to vines, peas and the like. Through Piedmont, Lombardy, Milan and Genoa the garden bean is a great article of culture, almost as much so as corn.

At Albenga is a rich plain opening from between two ridges of mountains, triangular to the sea and several miles long. Its growth is olives, figs, mulberries, vines, corn and beans. There is some pasture. This place is said to be rendered unhealthy in summer by the river which passes through the valley.

The wind continuing contrary, I took mules at Albenga for Oneglia. Along this tract are many of the tree called *carroubier*, being a species of locust. It is the *ceratonia siliqua* of Linnaeus. Its pods furnish food for horses and also for the poor in time of scarcity. It abounds in Naples and Spain. Oneglia and Port Maurice, which are within a mile of each other, are considerable places and in a rich country. At Saint Remo, an abundance of oranges and lemons and some palm trees.

FRANCE

R*ETURN TO PROVENCE*

*Fine trout in the stream of Vaucluse,
and the valley abounds with nightingales.*

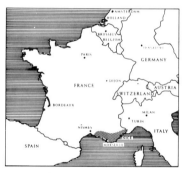

At Bordighera, between Ventimiglia and Menton, are extensive plantations of palms on the hill as well as in the plain. They bring fruit, but it does not ripen. Something is made of the midrib which is in great demand at Rome on the Palm Sunday and which renders this tree profitable here. From Menton to Monaco, more good land and extensive groves of oranges and lemons. Orange water sells here at forty sous the American quart.

A superb road might be made along the margin of the sea from Laspeze, where the level country of Italy opens, to Nice, where the Alps go off northwardly and the post roads of France begin. It might even follow the margin of the sea quite to Cette. By this road travelers would enter Italy without crossing the Alps, and all the little insulated villages of Genoa would communicate together and in time form one continued village along that road.

From le Luc to la Galinière lie long, small mountains, very rocky, with reddish soil, from bad to middling, mostly in olives, grapes, mulberries, vines and corn. Brignoles is in an extensive plain between two ridges of mountains and along a watercourse. I cross a mountain, low and easy, to Pourcieux.

The country is rocky and poor. To la Galinière are waving grounds bounded by mountains of rock at a little distance. There are some enclosures of dry wall from le Luc to la Galinière, also sheep and hogs. There is snow on the high mountains. I see no plums in the vicinities of Brignoles, which makes me conjecture that the celebrated plum of that name is not derived from this place.

Orgon is on the Durance River, and from there the plain opens till it becomes common with that of the Rhine so that from Orgon to Avignon is entirely a plain of rich, dark loam, in willows, mulberries, vines, corn and pasture. A very few figs, but I see no olives in this plain. Probably the cold winds have too much power here.

From the Bac de Nova, where I cross the Durance, to Avignon is about nine miles and from the same Bac to Vaucluse, eleven miles. In the valley of Vaucluse and on the hills impending over it are olive trees. The stream issuing from the fountain of Vaucluse is about twenty yards wide, four or five feet deep, and of such rapidity that it could not be stemmed by a canoe.

They are now mowing hay and gathering mulberry leaves. The high mountains just back of Vaucluse are covered with snow. Fine trout in the stream of Vaucluse, and the valley abounds with nightingales. Some good plains between Avignon and Remoulins, but generally hills, stony and poor, in olives, mulberries, vines and corn. Where it is waste the growth is box, furze, thyme and rosemary.

The white wine of Monsieur de Rochegude of Avignon resembles dry Lisbon. He sells it at six years old for twenty-two sous the bottle, the price of the bottle and cork included.

L A N G U E D O C

*The encroachments by the men on the offices proper
for the women is a great derangement in the order of things.*

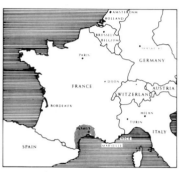

From Nîmes to Lunel I
see hills on the right and
plains on the left. The soil is
reddish, a little stony and of
middling quality, mostly in
olives, mulberries, vines and
corn. Lunel is famous for its
vin de muscat blanc, called
Lunel, or *vin muscat de Lunel*. It is made from muscat
grapes without fermenting
them in the hopper, which injures the quality. When a red
muscat is required, they prefer coloring it with a little Alicante
wine. The white is best. Two hundred and forty bottles, after being properly drawn off from the lees and ready for
bottling, costs from 120 to 200 livres for the first quality and
most recent vintage. It cannot be bought old, the demand
being sufficient to take it all the first year. Not more than from
3,000 to 6,000 gallons a year is made of this first quality.

A *setterie* yields about two-hundred fifty bottles, and my
informer supposes there are about two *setteries* in an acre.
The best harvests are those of Monsieur Bouquet and Monsieur Tremoulet. The vines are in rows four feet apart every
way.

There are two kinds of muscat grapes of which the wine
is made. The first has red skin but a white juice. If it be fermented on the skin, the coloring matter, which resides in
the skin, is imparted to the wine. If not fermented in that
way, the wine is white. Of the white grape only a white wine
can be made.

At Frontignan there are some tolerably good plains in

olives, vines, corn, sainfoin and lucerne. A great proportion of the hills is waste. There are some enclosures of stone and some sheep.

They cultivate a great deal of madder *(rubia tinctorum)* here, which is said to be immensely profitable. The first four years of madder are unproductive. The fifth and sixth years yield the whole value of the land. Then it must be renewed.

The species of sainfoin cultivated here by the name *sparsette* is the *hedysarum onobryches*. The *sparsette* is the common or true sainfoin. It lasts about five years. In the best land it is cut twice, in May and September, and yields 1,000 pounds of dry hay to an acre and 500 pounds the second year. Lucerne is the best of all forage; it is sowed widely here and lasts about twelve or fourteen years. It is cut four times a year, and an acre yields just under 2,000 pounds of dry hay from the four cuttings.

The territory in which the *vin muscat de Frontignan* is made is about three and a half miles long and one mile broad. The soil is reddish and stony, often containing as much stone as soil. On the left it is plain; on the right, hills.

About 250,000 bottles are produced annually, of which 150,000 are of the first quality, made on the *côteaux* [hillsides]. Of these, Madame Soubeinan makes 50,000; Monsieur Reboulle, 22,500; Monsieur Lambert, doctor of medicine on the faculty of Montpelier, 15,000; Monsieur Thomas, 12,500; Monsieur Argilliers, 12,500; Monsieur Audibert, 10,000; and there are some small proprietors who make the remainder.

The first quality is sold, brut, for 120 livres the lot of 250 bottles, but it is then thick and must have a winter and the *fouet* to render it potable and brilliant. The *fouet* is like a chocolate mill, the handle of iron, the brush of stiff hair.

In bottles this wine costs twenty-four sous. It is potable the April after it is made, is best that year, and after ten years begins to have a pitchy taste, resembling it to Malaga. It is not permitted to ferment more than half a day because it would not be so liquorish. The best color, and its natural one, is amber. By force of whipping it is made white, but loses flavor.

There are but 500 to 750 bottles made a year of red muscat, there being but one vineyard of the red grape, which belongs to a baker called Pascal. This sells in bottles at thirty sous, the bottle included.

Rondelle, a wine dealer, Porte St. Bernard, Fauxbourg St. Germains, Paris, buys 75,000 bottles of the first quality every year. The *côteaux* yield about 250 bottles the acre, while the plains yield 500. The inferior quality is not at all esteemed. It is bought by the merchants of Sète, as is also the wine of Béziers, and sold by them for Frontignan of the first quality. They sell 30,000 *pièces* a year under that name. The town of Frontignan marks its casks with a hot iron. An individual of that place having two empty casks was offered forty livres for them by a merchant of Sète.

An acre of good vineyard sells for from 650 to 1,000 livres and rents for 50 livres. A laboring man hires at 150 livres the year and is fed and lodged; a woman at half as much. Wheat sells at 10 livres for 100 pounds. They make some Indian corn here, which is eaten by the poor. The olives do not extend northward of this into the country more than fifty to sixty miles. In general, the olive country in Languedoc is about sixty miles broad. More of the waste land between Frontignan and Mirval is capable of culture, but it is marshy country, very subject to fever and ague and generally unhealthy. Thence arises, as is said, a want of hands.

Sète, a town of about ten thousand inhabitants, has as its principal commerce wine. It furnishes great quantities of grape pomace for making *verdigrise* [used in dyes and drugs]. They have a very growing commerce, but it is kept under by the privileged of Marseilles.

On the right of the Étang de Thau [Sound of Thau], near Agde, are plains of some width, then hills, in olives, vines, mulberry, corn and pasture. On the left a narrow sandbar separates the sound from the sea, along which it is proposed to make a road from Sète to Agde. The new road would lead from Montpelier by Sète and Agde to Béziers and would be more level and an hour or an hour and a half quicker.

The soil of both hill and plain is red in the country from Agde to Béziers. But at Béziers the country becomes hilly and is in olives, sainfoin, pasture, some vines and mulberries.

From Argilliers to Saumal are considerable plantations of vines. Those on the red hills to the right are said to produce good wine. The canal of Languedoc [Canal du Midi], along which I now travel, is a dozen yards wide at bottom, and twenty yards at the surface of the water, which is six feet deep. The barks which navigate it are seventy and eighty feet long and seventeen or eighteen feet wide. They are drawn by one horse and worked by two hands, one of whom is generally a woman. The locks are mostly kept by women, but the necessary operations are much too laborious for them.

The encroachments by the men on the offices proper for the women is a great derangement in the order of things. Men are shoemakers, tailors, upholsterers, cooks, housekeepers, housecleaners, bed makers. To live, the women are therefore obliged to undertake the offices that the men abandon. They become porters, carters, reapers, sailors, lockkeepers, smiters on the anvil and cultivators of the earth. Can we wonder if such of them as have a little beauty prefer easier courses to get their livelihood as long as that beauty lasts? For every man whom they thus employ, some girl, whose place he has thus taken, is driven to whoredom.

The passage of the eight locks at Béziers — that is, from the opening of the first to the last gate — took one hour and thirty-three minutes. The bark in which I go is about thirty-five feet long, drawn by one horse, and goes from two to three miles an hour. The canal yields an abundance of carp and eel. I see also small fish resembling our perch and chub. Some plants of white clover and some of yellow are found on the banks of the canal near Capestang, santolina also, and a great deal of yellow iris. The extensive and numerous fields of sainfoin in general bloom are beautiful.

From Saumal to Carcassonne I have always the river Aube close on my left. This river runs in the valley between the Cévennes and Pyrénées, serving as the common receptacle for both their waters. It is from 50 to 150 yards wide, always rapid, rocky and insusceptible of navigation. The canal passes on the side of hills made by the river, overlooks the river itself and its plains, and has its prospect ultimately terminated on one side by mountains of rock overtopped by the Pyrénées; on the other, by small mountains, sometimes of rock, sometimes of soil, overtopped by the Cévennes.

Marseillette is on a ridge which separates the river Aube

from the Étang de Marseillette. The canal in its approach to this village recrosses the ridge and resumes its general ground in front of the Aube. The land is in corn, sainfoin, pasture, vines, mulberries, willows and olives.

Opposite to Carcassonne, the canal receives the river Fresquel, about thirty yards wide, which is its substantial supply of water from here to Béziers. From Béziers to Agde, the river Orb furnishes it, and the Eraut, from Agde to the Étang de Thau. Where the Fresquel enters the canal, there is on the opposite side a waste to let off the superfluous waters. The horseway is continued over this waste by a stone bridge of eighteen arches.

I observed them fishing in the canal with a skimming net of about fifteen feet in diameter, with which they tell me they catch carp. Flax is in blossom, but neither strawberries nor peas can be found yet at Carcassonne. The Windsor bean has just come to table.

From the lock of la Lande I see the last olive trees near a farmhouse called la Lande. On a review of what I have seen and heard of this tree, the following seem to be its northern limits. Beginning on the Atlantic, at the Pyrénées, and along them to the meridian of la Lande, or of Carcassone; up that meridian to the Cévennes, as they begin just there to raise themselves high enough to afford the tree shelter. Along the Cévennes, to the parallel of forty-five degrees (crossing the Rhône near the mouth of the Isère), to the Alps. There, along the Alps and Apennines, to what parallel of latitude I know not.

The tracing here of the line becomes the most interesting. From the Atlantic, so far, the production of olives is the effect of shelter and latitude combined. But where does the tree venture to launch alone? Where, for instance, does its northern limit cross the Adriatic? I learn that the olive tree resists cold to fourteen above zero of Fahrenheit and that the orange resists to twenty-three degrees above zero of Fahrenheit.

Between Saint-Feriol, Escamaze and Lampy the country is almost entirely in waste. Some of it in shrubbery. Around Castelnaudari the country is hilly, as it has been constantly from Béziers, and is very rich. Where it is plain or nearly plain, the soil is black. In general, however, it is hilly and reddish and in corn. They cultivate a great deal of Indian corn here, which they call millet.

*M*IDI

It is remarkable that all the rivers running into the
Mediterranean are obstructed at their entrance by
bars and shallows, which often change their position. . . .
Other proofs that the land gains there on the sea are that
the towns of Saint Gilles and Notre Dame d'Asposts,
formerly seaports, are now far from the sea.

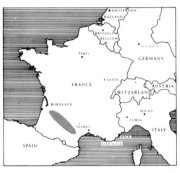

At Naurouze is the highest ground which the canal had to pass between the two seas. It became necessary then to find water still higher to bring it here. The springs of the most western branches of the river Fresquel, in the Montagnes Noires, a considerable distance off to the eastward, were brought together and conducted to Naurouze, where that river's waters are divided, part furnishing the canal towards the ocean, the rest towards the Mediterranean as far as the lock of Fresquel. There, as has been before noted, the Lampy's branch and the Alzau, under the name of the Fresquel, enter.

They have found that a lock of six feet is best; however, eight feet is well enough. Beyond this length, it is bad. Monsieur Pin tells me of a lock of thirty feet, made in Sweden, of which it was impossible to open the gates. They therefore divided it into four locks. The small gates of the locks of this canal at Naurouze have six square feet of surface. They tried the machinery of the jack for opening them. They were more easily opened than before, but very subject to being deranged, however strongly made. They returned therefore to the original wooden screw, which is excessively slow and laborious.

I calculate that five minutes are lost at every basin by this screw, which is one-eighth of the time necessary to navigate the canal. If a method of lifting the gate at one stroke could be found, it would reduce the passage from eight to seven days and the freight equally. I suggested to Monsieur Pin and others a quadrantal gate, turning on a pivot and lifted by a lever like a pump handle and aided by a windlass and cord, if necessary. He will try it and inform me of the success.

An idea for a canal lock gate.

Two hundred forty barks, the largest of 100 tons, suffice to perform the business of this canal, which is stationary, having neither increased nor diminished for many years. When pressed, they can pass and repass between Toulouse and Béziers in fourteen days, but sixteen is the common period. The canal is navigated ten and a half months of the year, the other month and a half being necessary to lay it dry, clean it and repair the works. This is done in July and August, when there would perhaps be a want of water.

From Baziege to Toulouse the country continues hilly but very rich. It is in mulberries, willows, some vines, corn, maize, pasture, beans and flax. A great number of châteaux and good houses in the neighborhood of the canal. The people are partly in farmhouses, partly in villages. I suspect the farmhouses are occupied by the farmers, while the laborers (who are mostly by the day) reside in the villages. Near the latter are some fields of yellow clover.

At Toulouse the canal ends. It has four communications with the Mediterranean. First, through the sounds of Thau, Frontignan, Palavas, Maguelone, and Manjo, the Canal de la Radela Aiguesmortes, the Canal des Salines de Pecair and the arm of the Rhône called "bras de fer," which ends at Fourgues, opposite to Arles, and thence down the Rhône.

Second, at Sète, by a canal of a few hundred yards, leading out of the Étang de Thau into the sea. The vessels pass the sound, through a length of ten miles, with sails.

Third, at Agde, by the river Eraut, three miles long. It has but five or six feet of water at its mouth. It is joined to the canal at the upper part of this communication by a branch of a canal 180 yards long.

Fourth, at Narbonne, by a canal they are now opening, which leads from the great canal near the aqueduct of the river Cesse, three miles long, into the Aude. This new canal will have five locks each of about a twelve-foot fall. Vessels will cross the Aude very obliquely and descend a branch of it twenty miles, through four lock-basins, to Narbonne and from Narbonne down the same branch, four miles into the Étang de Sigen, across it four and half miles, issuing at an inlet called Grau de la Nouvelle into the Gulf of Lyons. But only vessels of thirty or forty tons can enter this inlet.

Of these four combinations, only that of Sète leads to a deep seaport because the exit is there by a canal and not by a river. Those by the Rhône, Eraut and Aude are blocked up by bars at the mouths of those rivers. It is remarkable that all the rivers running into the Mediterranean are obstructed at their entrance by bars and shallows, which often change their position.

Indeed, the formation of these bars seems not confined to the mouths of the rivers, though certainly it takes place at them. Along almost the whole of the coast, from Marseilles towards the Pyrénées, banks of sand are thrown up, parallel with the coast, which have insulated portions of the sea and formed them into ponds, or sounds, through which here and there narrow and shallow inlets only are preserved by the currents of the rivers. These sounds fill up in time with the mud and sand deposited in them by the rivers. Thus, the Étang de Vendres, navigated formerly by vessels of sixty tons, is now nearly filled up by the mud and sands of the Aude.

Other proofs that the land gains there on the sea are that the towns of Saint-Gilles and Notre Dame d'Aposts, formerly seaports, are now far from the sea. Aiguesmortes, where are still to be seen the iron rings to which vessels were formerly moored, and where Saint Louis embarked for Palestine, has now in its vicinities only ponds which cannot be navigated and communicates with the sea by an inlet called Grau du Roy, though which only fishing barks can pass. It is pretty well established that all the delta of Egypt has been formed by the depositions of the Nile and the alluvions of the sea, and it is probable that that operation is still going on. Has this peculiarity of the Mediterrenean any connection with the scantiness of its tides, which even at the equinoxes are of two or three feet only?

The communication from the western end of the canal to the ocean is by the river Garonne. It has been proposed to open a canal to the Tarn from Toulouse, along the right side of the river.

BORDEAUX

*Desgrands, a wine broker, tells me they never mix
the wines of first quality, but that they mix
the inferior ones to improve them.*

The Garonne and rivers emptying into it make extensive and rich plains, which are in mulberries, willows, corn, maize, pasture, beans and flax. The hills are in corn, maize, beans and a considerable proportion of vines. There is a great deal of forage they call *farouche*. It is a species of red trefoil, with few leaves, a very coarse stalk, and a cylindrical blossom of two inches in length and three-quarters of an inch in diameter, consisting of floscules, exactly as does that of the red clover. It seems to be a coarse food, but very plentiful. They say it is for their oxen. These are very fine, large and cream-colored. The services of the farm and of transportation are performed chiefly by them. There are a few horses and asses but no mules.

Even in the city of Bordeaux, I see scarcely any beasts of draught but oxen. Crossing the Garonne at Langon, I find the plains entirely of sand and gravel, and they continue so to Bordeaux. Where they are capable of anything, they are in vines, which are in rows — four, five, or six feet apart and sometimes more. Near Langon is Sauterne, where the best white wines of Bordeaux are made. The waste lands are in fern, furze, shrubbery and dwarf trees. The farmers live on their farms.

At Agen, Castres and Bordeaux, strawberries and peas are now brought to table, so that the country on the canal of Languedoc seems to have later seasons than that east and west of it. What can be the cause? To the eastward the protection of the Cévennes makes the warm season advance sooner. Does the neighborhood of the Mediterranean cooperate? And does that of the ocean mollify and advance the season to the westward? There are ortolans at Agen but none at Bordeaux.

The buildings on the canal and the Garonne are mostly of brick, the size of the bricks the same with that of the ancient Roman brick seen in the remains of their buildings in this country. In those of a circus at Bordeaux, considerable portions of which are standing, I measured the bricks and found them nineteen or twenty inches long, eleven or twelve inches wide, and from one and a half to two inches thick, their texture as fine, compact and solid as that of porcelain. The bricks now made, though of the same dimensions, are not so fine. They are burnt in a kind of furnace and make excellent work. The elm tree shows itself at Bordeaux, peculiarly proper for being spread flat for arbors. Many are done in this way on the Quay des Charterons.

The cantons in which the most celebrated wines of Bordeaux are made are Médoc down the river, Grave adjoining the city, and the parishes next above; all are on the same side of the river.

In the first is made red wine principally; in the two last, white. In Médoc they plant the vines in cross rows of three and a half feet. They keep them so low that poles extended along the rows one way, horizontally, about fifteen or eighteen inches above the ground serve to tie the vines to and leave the cross row open to the plough.

In Grave they set the plants in quincunxes — in other words, in equilateral triangles of three and a half feet every side — and they stick a pole of six or eight feet high to every vine separately. The vine stock is sometimes three or four feet high. They find these two methods equal in culture, duration, quantity and quality. The former, however, admits the alternatives of tending by hand or with the plough.

The grafting of the vine, although a critical operation, is practiced with success. When the graft has taken, they bend it into the earth and let it take root above the scar. The new vines begin to yield an indifferent wine at three years old but not a good one till twenty-five years, nor after eighty, when they begin to yield less and worse and must be renewed.

They dung a little in Médoc and Grave because of the poverty of the soil, but very little, as more would affect the wine. The vineyards of first quality are all worked by their proprietors. They employ a kind of overseer at four or five hundred livres the year, finding him lodging and drink; but he feeds himself. He superintends and directs, though he is expected to work but little. If the proprietor has a garden, the overseer tends that.

They never hire laborers by the year. The day wages for a man are thirty sous, a woman's fifteen sous, both feeding themselves. The women make the bundles of sarments [vine cuttings], weed, pull off the snails, tie the vines and gather the grapes. During the vintage they are paid high and fed well.

For red wines, there are four vineyards of the first quality: Château Margaux, belonging to the Marquis d'Agicourt, who makes about a hundred fifty *tonneau* [100 cases], of 1,000 bottles each. He has engaged to Jernon, a merchant.

La Tour de Ségur [Château Latour], in Saint-Lambert, belonging to Monsieur Miresmenil, who makes 125 *tonneaux*.

Haut-Brion, belonging two-thirds to the Count de Fumel, who has engaged to Barton, a merchant. The other third belongs to Count de Toulouse, at Toulouse. The whole is 75 *tonneaux*.

Château Lafite, belonging to the President Pichard [president of a regional council], at Bordeaux, who makes 175 *tonneaux*.

The wines of the three first are not in perfection till four years old. Those of Lafite, being somewhat lighter, are good at three years; that is to say, the crop of 1786 is good in the spring of 1789.

The growths of the year 1783 sell now at 2,000 livres the *tonneau*; those of 1784, on account of the superior quality of that vintage, sell at 2,400 livres; those of 1785, at 1,800 livres; those of 1786, at 1,800 livres, though they had sold at first for only 1,500 livres.

Red wines of the second quality are Rausan-Segala,

Léoville, Gruand Larose, Kinvan, Durfort Vivens. The third class are Calon Ségur, Mouton, Rauzan, Gassie, Arboete, Pontet, Canet, Marquis de Freme, Gandalle. After these, they are reckoned common wines and sell from 500 livres down to 120 livres the *tonneau*. All red wines decline after a certain age, losing color, flavor and body. Those of Bordeaux begin to decline at about seven years old.

Of white wines, those made in the canton of Grave are most esteemed at Bordeaux. The best crops are:

Pontac, which formerly belonged to Monsieur de Pontac but now to Monsieur de Lamont. He makes forty *tonneaux*, which sell at 400 livres a ton new. Monsieur de Lamont tells me he has a kind of grape without seeds, which I did not formerly suppose to exist.

Saint-Brice, belonging to Monsieur de Pontac. He makes thirty *tonneaux*, which sell at 350 livres a *tonneau* new. Le Carbonnieux, belonging to the Benedictine monks, who make fifty *tonneaux*. They never sell till it is three or four years old and get 800 livres the *tonneau*.

Those made in the three parishes next above Grave, and more esteemed at Paris, are:

Sauterne, the best crop belonging to Monsieur d'Yquem at Bordeaux, or to Count de Lur-Saluces, his son-in-law. They receive 100 livres old. The next best crop is Monsieur de Filotte's, 100 *tonneaux* in size and selling at the same price as the others.

Prignac, the best being President du Roy's at Bordeaux. He makes 175 *tonneaux*, which sell at 300 livres new and 600 livres, old. Those of 1784, for their extraordinary quality, sell at 800 livres.

Barsac, the best belonging to the President Pichard, who makes 150 *tonneaux*, at 280 livres new and 600 livres old.

Sauterne is the pleasantest, next Prignac, and lastly Barsac; and all are stronger than Grave. There are other good crops made in the same parishes of Sauterne, Prignac and Barsac but none as good as these.

There is a virgin wine which though made of a red grape is of a light rose color because — as it is made without pressure — the coloring matter of the skin does not mix with the juice. There are other wines, from the preceding prices down to seventy-five livres. In general, the white wines keep longest. They will be in perfection till fifteen or twenty years of age. The best vintage now to be bought is of 1784, both of red and white. There has been no other good year since 1779.

The celebrated vineyards before mentioned are in plains, as is generally the canton of Médoc and that of Grave. In particular, the soil of Haut-Brion, which I examined, is a sand in which is near as much round gravel or small stone and very little loam. This is also the general soil of Médoc. That of Pontac, which I examined also, is a little different. It is clayey, with a fourth or fifth of fine rotten stone, and at a depth of two feet it becomes all a rotten stone.

The principal English wine merchants at Bordeaux are Jemon, Barton, Johnston, Foster, Skinner, Copinger and Mac-Cartey. The chief French wine merchants are Feger, Nerac, Bruneau, Jauge and du Verget. Desgrands, a wine broker, tells me they never mix the wines of first quality, but that they mix the inferior ones to improve them. The smallest wines make the best brandy.

POITOU-CHARENTES

*There are more and better trees than I have seen
in all my journey — a great many apple and cherry trees.*

From Bordeaux to Blaye the country near the river is hilly, chiefly in vines, some corn and some pasture. Further out are plains, boggy and waste. To Etaulière, there are sometimes boggy plains, sometimes waving grounds; the country is sandy, always poor, generally waste, in fern and furze with some corn. To Mirambeau and Saint-Génis, it is hilly, poor and mostly waste. There is some corn and maize, however, and better trees than usual. Towards Pons the soil becomes a little red and is mostly rotten stone. There are vines, corn and maize. At Pons the country becomes better, a blackish mold mixed with a rotten, chalky stone. A great many vines and corn, maize and *farouche* can be seen. From Lajart to Saintes and Rochefort, the soil is reddish, its foundation a chalky rock at about a foot's depth; it is also in vines, corn, maize, clover, alfalfa and pasture. There are more and better trees than I have seen in all my journey — a great many apple and cherry trees.

From Rochefort to la Rochelle it is sometimes hilly and red, with a chalky foundation, middling good, in corn, pasture and some waste. Sometimes it is reclaimed marsh, in clover and corn, except the parts accessible to the tide, which are in wild grass.

Around la Rochelle it is a low plain. Towards Usseau and halfway to Marais are level highlands with red soil, mixed with an equal quantity of broken chalk, mostly in vines, some corn and pasture. To Marais and halfway to Saint-Hermine, it is reclaimed marsh, dark, tolerably good and all in pasture. There I rise to plains a little higher, red, with a chalky foundation, boundless to the eye and altogether in corn and maize.

At Saint-Hermine the country becomes very hilly, a red clay mixed with chalky stone, generally waste, in furze and broom, with some patches of corn and maize, and so it continues to Chantonnay and Saint-Fulgent. Through the whole of this road from Bordeaux are frequent hedgerows and small patches of forest wood, not good, yet better than I have seen in the preceding part of my journey. Towards Montaigu the soil mends a little. The cultivated parts are in corn and pasture, the uncultivated in broom. It is in very small enclosures of ditch and quickset.

BRITTANY

The villages announce a general poverty, as does
every other appearance. Women smite on the anvil
and work with the hoe, and cows are yoked to labor.

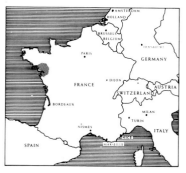

From approaching the Loire to Nantes the country is more level. The soil from Rochelle to this place may be said to have been sometimes red, but oftener gray and always on a chalky foundation. The last census, of about 1770, found 120,000 inhabitants at Nantes. They conjecture there are now 150,000, which equals it to Bordeaux.

The country from Nantes to Lorient is very hilly and poor, the soil gray, and nearly half is waste, in furze and broom, among which is some poor grass. The cultivated parts are in corn, some maize, a good many apple trees, but no vines. All is in small enclosures of quickset hedge and ditch. There are patches and hedgerows of forest wood, not quite deserving the name of timber. The people are mostly in villages. They eat rye bread and are ragged. The villages announce a general poverty, as does every other appearance. Women smite on the anvil and work with the hoe, and cows are yoked to labor. There are great numbers of cattle, insomuch that butter is their staple. I saw neither asses nor mules, yet it is said that the fine mules I have met with on my journey are raised in Poictou.

There are but few châteaux here. I observe mill ponds and hoes with long handles. Have they not, in common with us, derived these from England, of which Brittany is probably a colony? Lorient is supposed to contain 25,000 inhabitants. They tell me here that to make a reasonable profit on potash and pearl ash, as bought in America, the former should sell at thirty livres, the latter thirty-six livres the quintal. Of turpentine they make no use in their vessels. Bayonne furnishes pitch enough, but tar is in demand, and America's sells well.

The tower of Lorient is 65 feet above the level of the sea, 120 feet high, 25 feet in diameter. It cost 30,000 livres, besides the materials of the old tower.

The country and produce from Lorient to Rennes and from Rennes to Nantes are precisely similar to those from Nantes to Lorient. Around Rennes it is somewhat more level, perhaps less poor, and almost entirely in pasture. The soil is always gray. Some small separate houses which seem to be the residences of laborers or very small farmers. The walls are frequently made of mud and the roofs generally covered with slate.

I have heard no nightingale since the last day of May.

A gate seen in Brittany

There are gates in this country made in such a manner that the top rail of the gate overshoots backwards the hind post so as to counterpoise the gate and prevent its swagging.

Vessels of eight feet draught only can come to Nantes. Those which are larger lie at Point Boeuf, forty miles below Nantes and twenty miles above the mouth of the river. There is a continued navigation from Nantes to Paris, through the Loire, the Canal de Briare and the Seine.

Carolina rice is preferred to that of Lombardy for the Guinea trade because it requires less water to boil it.

A *NJOU*

There is very good wine made on these hills,
not equal indeed to the Bordeaux of best quality,
but to that of good quality and like it. It is a great
article of exportation from Anjou and Touraine and
probably is sold abroad, under the name of Bordeaux.

Ascending the Loire from Nantes, the road, as far as Angers, leads over the hills, which are gray, more often below than above mediocrity, and in corn, pasture, vines, some maize, flax and hemp. There are no waste lands. Around the limits of Brittany and Anjou, which are between Loriottiere and Saint-George, the lands change for the better. Here and there I get views of the plains on the Loire; of some extent and of a good appearance, they are in corn and pasture. After passing Angers, the road is raised out of the reach of inundations, which at the same time wards them off from the interior plains. It passes generally along the river's side but sometimes leads through the plains, which, after I pass Angers, become extensive and good, in corn, pasture, some maize, hemp, flax, peas and beans. Many willows, also poplars and walnuts can be seen.

Some broom here still, on which the cattle and sheep browse in winter and spring, when they have no other green food; the hogs eat the blossoms and pods in spring and summer. This blossom, though disagreeable when smelt in a small quantity, is of delicious fragrance when there is a whole field of it.

There are some considerable vineyards on the river plains

just before Les Trois Volées, and after that, where the hills on the left come into view, the plains are mostly in vines. Their soil is clayey and stony, a little reddish, and of southern aspect. The hills on the other side of the river, to the north, are not in vines. There is very good wine made on these hills, not equal indeed to the Bordeaux of best quality, but equal to that of good quality and like it. It is a great article of exportation from Anjou and Touraine and probably is sold abroad under the name of Bordeaux.

All along both hills of the Loire is a mass of white stone, not durable, growing black with time and so soft that the people cut their houses out of the solid face of the hills making partitions, chimneys and doors. The hillsides resemble coney burrows, full of inhabitants. The borders of the Loire are almost a continued village. There are many châteaux, many cattle, sheep, horses and some asses.

*T*OURAINE

Monsieur du Verget, a physician of Tours, of great science and candor, . . .was perfectly in sentiment with Monsieur de la Sauvagiere, that not only the Faluniere, but many other places about Tours, would convince any unbiased observer that shells are a fruit of the earth, spontaneously produced.

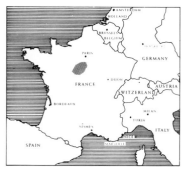

Being desirous of inquiring here into a fact stated by Voltaire in his *Questions Encyclopédiques*, in the articles "Coquilles," relative to the growth of shells unconnected with animal bodies, I called on Monsieur Gentil, first secretary of the region's administrator, at the château of Monsieur de la Sauvagière, near Tours. The administrator had written to him on my behalf at the request of the Marquis de Chastellux.

I stated to him the fact as advanced by Voltaire and found he was, of all men, the best to whom I could have addressed myself. He told me he had been in correspondence with Voltaire on that very subject and was perfectly acquainted with Monsieur de la Sauvagière and the Falunière, where the fact is said to have taken place. That place is at the Château de Grillemont, twenty-four miles from Tours, on the road to Bordeaux, and belongs now to Monsieur d'Orcai.

He said that de la Sauvagière was a man of truth and might be relied on for whatever facts he stated as of his own observations. But, he added, de la Sauvagière was overcharged with imagination, which, in matters of opinion and theory, often led him beyond his facts. This feature in his character had appeared principally in what he wrote on the antiquities of Touraine. As to the fact in question, however, he believed him.

Monsieur Gentil said he himself, indeed, had not watched the same shells growing from small to great, as Sauvagière had done, but he had often seen such masses of those shells of all sizes, from a point to a full size, as to carry conviction to his mind that they were in the act of growing. He had once made a collection of shells for the emperor's cabinet, reserving duplicates of them for himself. These afforded proofs of the same fact. Afterwards he gave those duplicates to a Monsieur du Verget, a physician of Tours, of great science and candor, who was collecting on a larger scale and who was perfectly in sentiment with Monsieur de la Sauvagière, that not only the Falunière, but many other places about Tours, would convince any unbiased observer that shells are a fruit of the earth, spontaneously produced.

He gave me a copy of de la Sauvagière's *Recueil de dissertations*, presented by the author, wherein is one essay *Sur la vegetation spontanée des coquilles du Château des Places*. So far, I repeat from him, what are we to conclude? That we have not materials enough yet to form any conclusion. The fact stated by Sauvagière is not against any law of nature and is therefore possible. But it is so little analogous to her habitual processes that, if true, it would be extraordinary.

He continues that to command our belief, therefore, there should be such a suite of observations as that their untruth would be more extraordinary than the existence of the fact they affirm. The bark of trees, the skin of fruits and animals, the feathers of birds, receive their growth and nutriment from the internal circulation of a juice through the vessels of the individual they cover. We conclude from analogy, then, that the shells of the testaceous tribe receive also their growth from a like internal circulation — if it be urged that this does not exclude the possibility of a like shell being produced by the passage of a fluid through the pores of the circumjacent body, whether of earth, stone or water.

I answer that it is not within the usual economy of nature to use two processes for one species of production. While I withold my assent, however, from this hypothesis, I must also deny it to every other I have ever seen by which their authors pretend to account for the origin of shells in high places. Some of these are against the laws of nature and therefore impossible. Others are built on positions more difficult to assent to than that of de la Sauvagière. They all suppose the shells to have covered submarine animals and have then to answer the question: How came they 15,000 feet above the level of the sea? And they answer it by demanding what cannot be conceded.

As one, therefore, who had rather have no opinion than a false one, I will suppose this question to be among those beyond the investigation of human sagacity or wait till further and fuller observations enable me to decide it.

I heard a nightingale today at Chanteloup. The gardener says it is the male alone who sings while the female sits and that when the young are hatched he also ceases.

In the boudoir at Chanteloup is an ingenious contrivance to hide the projecting steps of a staircase. Three steps were of necessity to project into the boudoir. They therefore made triangular steps, and, instead of resting on the floor as usual, they are made fast at their broad end to the stair door, swinging out and in with that. When shut, it runs them under the other steps. When open, it brings them out to their proper place.

In the kitchen garden are three pumps worked by one horse. The pumps are placed in an equilateral triangle, each side of which is of about thirty-five feet. In the center is a post, ten or twelve feet high and one foot in diameter. In the top of this enters the bent end of a lev-

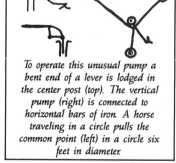

To operate this unusual pump a bent end of a lever is lodged in the center post (top). The vertical pump (right) is connected to horizontal bars of iron. A horse traveling in a circle pulls the common point (left) in a circle six feet in diameter.

er, about twelve or fifteen feet long, with a singletree at the other end. About three feet from the bent end, it receives on a pin three horizontal bars of iron, which at their other end lay hold of one corner of a quadrantal crank — like a bell crank — moving in a vertical plane. To the other corner of the crank is hooked the vertical handle of the pump. The crank turns on its point as a center by a pin or pivot passing through it. The horse moving the lever horizontally in a circle, every point of the lever describes a circle of six feet in diameter. It gives a stroke, then, of six feet to the handle of each pump at each revolution.

At Blois the road leaves the river and traverses the hills, which are mostly reddish, sometimes gray, and good enough to be in vines, corn and sainfoin. From Orleans to the river Juines, at Étampes, it is a continued plain of corn and sainfoin, tolerably good, sometimes gray, sometimes red. From Étampes to Estrechy, the country is mountainous and rocky, resembling that of Fontainbleau.

Part Two

NORTHERN TOUR
1788

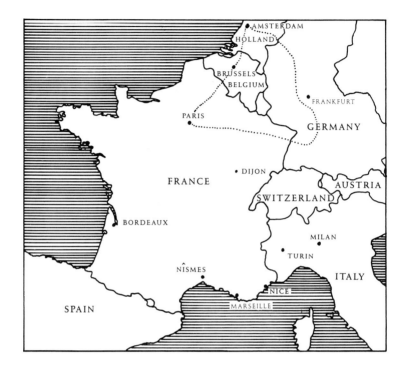

HOLLAND

AMSTERDAM

*Mr. Hermen Hend Damen, a merchant-broker of Amsterdam,
tells me that the emigrants to America come from the Palatinate
down the Rhine and take ship from Amsterdam. . . .
He says they might be had in any number to go to America
and settle lands as tenants or as sharecroppers.*

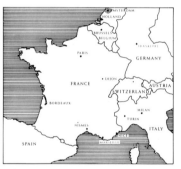

In Amsterdam a large number of unusual items caught my eye soon after arriving here.

The joists of houses, for example, are placed, not with their sides horizontal and perpendicular, but diamond wise. This is done, first of all, for greater strength; secondly, to support the brick arches that are used. Windows open so that they admit air and not rain. The upper sash opens on a horizontal axis or pins in the center of the sides, and the lower sash slides up.

The flagstaff on the mast of a vessel swivels on one bolt, while below is another bolt which is taken in and out to fasten it or to let it down. When taken out, the lower end of the staff is shoved out of its case and the upper end, being heavier, brings itself

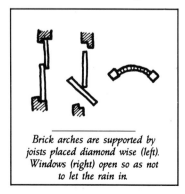

Brick arches are supported by joists placed diamond wise (left). Windows (right) open so as not to let the rain in.

down. A rope must have been previously fastened to the butt end to pull it down again when someone wanted to raise the flag end.

There is a machine for drawing light empty boats over a dam at Amsterdam. Sloping stages are attached to either side of the dam. A boat is presented to the stage, the rope of the axis made fast to it and the boat drawn up. The water on one side of the dam is about four feet higher than on the other.

The camels [watertight containers designed to raise ships] used for lightening ships will raise them eight feet. There are beams passing through the ships' sides, projecting to the outside of the camels and resting on them. Besides this, there are a great number of winches on the camels, the ropes of which are made fast to the gunwale of the ship. When the camel is placed alongside, water is let into it so as nearly to sink it. In this state it receives the beams of the ship, and then the water is pumped out.

I have seen, for the first time, wind sawmills here. They are built on a circular foundation of brick, raised about three or four feet high and covered with a curb of wood. Little rollers under the sill to make them turn easily on the curb. A hanging bridge projects at each end about fifteen or twenty feet beyond the circular area to increase the play of the timbers on the frame. The wings are at one side, and there is a shelter over the hanging bridges of very light plank with scarcely any frame.

I have also seen a bridge on a canal that turns on a swivel, by which means it is kept along the side of the canal so as not to be in the way of boats when it is not in use. When used, it is turned across the canal.

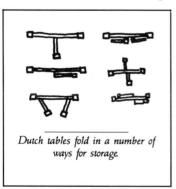

Dutch tables fold in a number of ways for storage.

Mr. Ameshoff, merchant at Amsterdam, has an aviary worthy of notice. Each kind of the large birds has a coop eight feet wide and four feet deep; the middle of the front is occupied by a broad glass window, on one side of which is a door for the keeper to enter at, and on the other a little trapdoor for the birds to pass in and out. The floor is strewed with clean hay. Before each coop is a court of eight to sixteen feet, with wire on the front and netting above, if the fowls in it are able to fly. For such as require it, there are bushes of evergreen growing in their court for them to lay their eggs under.

The coops are frequently divided into two stories. In the upper are those birds which perch, such as pidgeons, and in the lower are those which feed on the ground, such as pheasants and partridges. The court is in common for both stories, because the birds do no injury to each other. For the waterfowl there is a pond of water passing through the courts, with a movable separation. While they are breeding, they must be separate, afterwards they may come together. The small birds are some of them in a common aviary and some in cages.

Mr. Hermen Hend Damen, a merchant-broker of Amsterdam, tells me that the emigrants to America come from the Palatinate [a state of the old German empire] down the Rhine and take ship from Amsterdam. He says they might be had in any number to go to America and settle lands as tenants or as sharecroppers. Perhaps they could serve their employer one year as an indemnification for the passage and then be bound to remain on his lands seven years. They could come to Amsterdam at their own expense. He thinks they could employ more than fifty acres each, but who knows, especially if they have fifty acres for their wife also?

Baron Steuben, of this city, has been generally suspected of having first suggested the idea of the self-styled Society of the Cincinnati. But Mr. Adams tells me that in 1776 he had called at a tavern in the state of New York to dine just at the moment when the British army was landing at Frog's Neck. Generals Washington, Lee, Knox and Parsons came to the same tavern. Adams got into conversation with Knox. They talked of ancient history — of Fabius, who used to raise the Romans from the dust—and of the contest in progress at that time. General Knox, in the course of the conversation, said he should wish for some ribbon to wear in his hat or in his buttonhole that would be transmitted to his descendants as a badge and a proof that he had fought in defense of their liberties. He spoke of it in such precise terms as showed he had revolved it in his mind before.

Mr. Adams says he and Knox were standing together in the door of the tavern and does not recollect whether General Washington and the others were near enough to hear the conversation or were even in the room at that moment. Baron Steuben did not arrive in America till above a year after that.

I saw a remarkable house, called Hope's House, near Haarlem. It is said it will cost four tons of silver, or 40,000 pounds sterling. The separation between the middle building and wings in the upper story has a capricious appearance, yet a pleasing one. The right wing of the house (which is the left in the plan) extends back to a great length, so as to make the ground plan in the form of an *L*. The parapet has a panel of wall and a panel of ballusters alternately, which lighten it. There is no portico, the columns being backed against the wall of the front.

Hope's house near Haarlem.

GELDERLAND

*The canal is lined with country houses,
which bespeaks the wealth and cleanliness of the country.
But the houses are generally in an uncouth state
and exhibit no regular architecture.*

The lower parts of the low countries seem partly to have been gained from the sea and partly to be made up of the plains of the IJssel, the Rhine and the Maas united. To Utrecht nothing but plains, of a rich, black mold, wet and lower than the level of the waters which intersect them. They are almost entirely in grass with few or no farmhouses, as the business of grazing requires few laborers.

The canal is lined with country houses, which bespeaks the wealth and cleanliness of the country. But the houses are generally in an uncouth state and exhibit no regular architecture. After Utrecht the hills northeast of the Rhine come into view and gather in towards the river.

The plains there become more sandy. The hills, very poor and sandy, are generally waste, in broom and sometimes a little corn. The plains are in corn, grass and willows. The plantations of the latter are immense and give the place the air of an uncultivated country. There are now few châteaux, and farmhouses abound, built generally of brick and covered with tile or thatch. There are some apple trees but no forest. In the gardens are hedges of beech, one foot apart. Because they do not lose their old leaves until they are pushed off in the spring by the young ones, they give the shelter of evergreens.

The Rhine is here about three hundred yards wide. On the left side, the plains of the Rhine, the Rijn and the Waal unite. The Rhine and Waal are crossed on vibrating boats, the rope supported by a line of seven little barks. The platform by which you go onto the ferryboat is supported by pontoons.

A Dutch wheelbarrow is convenient for loading and unloading

The view from the hill at Cress is sublime. It commands the Waal and extends far up the Rhine. Also the view up and down the Waal from the Bellevue of Nijmeguen is very fine. The château here is pretended to have lodged Julius Caesar. This is giving it an antiquity of at least eighteen centuries, which must be apocryphal.

GERMANY

*W*ESTPHALIA

*Here the vines begin, it is the most northern spot
on the earth on which wine is made.*

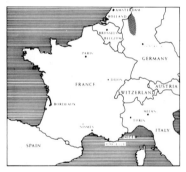

The transition from ease and opulence to extreme poverty is remarkable as one crosses the line between the Dutch and German territories. The soil and climate are the same — the governments alone differ. The poverty is visible; the fear of slaves is also visible in the faces of the German subjects.

The road leads generally over the hills but sometimes through skirts of the plains of the Rhine. These are always extensive and good. The hills are almost always sandy, barren, uncultivated and insusceptible of culture, covered with broom and moss. Here and there is a little indifferent forest, which is sometimes of beech. The plains are principally in corn and some grass and willow.

There are no châteaux, nor houses that bespeak the existence of even a middle class. Universal and equal poverty overspreads the whole. In the villages, too — which seem to be falling down — an overproportion of women is evident. The cultivators seem to live on their farms. The farmhouses are of mud, the better sort of brick, all covered over with thatch.

Kleve is little more than a village. If there are shops or magazines of merchandise in it, they show little. Here and there at a window some small articles are hung up within the glass.

I crossed the Rhine at Essenberg. It is there about a quarter of a mile wide, or five hundred yards. It is crossed in a scow with sails. The wind coming from behind, I was eight or ten minutes only in the passage.

Duisburg is but a walled-in village whose buildings are mostly brick. No new ones to indicate a thriving state. I had understood that near Duisburg were remains of the encampment of Varus, in which he and his legions fell by the arms of Arminius (in the time of Tiberius, I think it was), but there was not a person to be found in Duisburg who could understand either English, French, Italian or Latin. So I could make no inquiry.

From Duisburg to Düsseldorf the road leads sometimes over the hills, sometimes through the plains of the Rhine, the quality of which are as before described. On the hills, however, are considerable groves of oak, of spontaneous growth, which seem to be more than a century old. The soil being barren, however, the trees are crooked and knotty. The undergrowth is broom and moss. In the plains it is corn entirely, as they are become rather sandy for grass.

There are no enclosures on the Rhine at all. The houses are poor and ruinous, mostly a mixture of brick and scantling [small pieces of timber]. A good deal of grape is cultivated.

The plains from Düsseldorf to Cologne are much more extensive and go off in barren downs at some distance from the river. These downs extend far, according to appearance. They are manuring the plains with lime. I cross at Cologne on a pendulum boat.

A gate at the elector's chateau on the road between Dusseldorf and Cologne.

I observe that the hog of this country (Westphalia), of which the celebrated ham is made, is tall, gaunt, and has heavy lop ears. Fatted at a year old, it weighs 100 or 120 pounds; at two years old, 200 pounds. Their principal food is acorns. About 4 pounds of fine Holland salt is put on

100 pounds of pork. They find that a small hog makes the sweetest meat. It is smoked in a room which has no chimney. Well-informed people here tell me there is no other part of the world where the bacon is smoked. They do not know that we do it.

Cologne is a sovereign city, having no territory out of its walls. It contains about sixty thousand inhabitants, appears to have much commerce, and to abound with poor. Its commerce is principally in the hands of Protestants, of whom there are about sixty houses in the city. They are extremely restricted in their operations and otherwise oppressed in every form by the government, which is Catholic and excessively intolerant. Some time ago their senate, by a majority of twenty-two to eighteen, allowed them to have a church. But it is believed this privilege will be revoked. There are about two hundred fifty Catholic churches in the city.

Here the vines begin; it is the most northern spot on the earth on which wine is made. Their first grapes came from Orleans; since then they have come from Alsace and Champagne. It is thirty-two years only since the first vines were sent from here to the Cape of Good Hope, of which the Cape wine is now made. Afterwards new supplies were sent from the same quarter. That, I suppose, is the most southern spot on the globe where wine is made. It is singular that the same vine should have furnished two wines as much opposed to each other in quality as in situation.

I saw many walnut trees today in the open fields. It would seem as if this tree and wine require the same climate. The soil begins now to be reddish, both on the hills and in the plains. The plains from Cologne to Bonn extend about three miles from the river on each side, but a little above Bonn they become contracted and continue thence to be from one mile to nothing, comprehending both sides of the river. They are in corn, some clover and rape [a plant whose leaves are used for food for hogs] and many vines.

The vines are planted in rows three feet apart both ways. They are left about six or eight feet high and stuck with poles ten or twelve feet high. To these poles they are tied in two places, at the height of about two and four feet. The hills are generally excessively steep, a great proportion of them barren. The rest is in vines principally, sometimes in small patches of corn. I observed that they dung their vines plentifully in the plains — although the soil is rich — but note that here, as elsewhere, the plains yield much wine, but bad. The good is furnished from the hills.

Andernach is the port on the Rhine to which the famous millstones of Cologne are brought. The quarries are actually twelve to sixteen miles from here. I suppose they have been called Cologne millstones because the merchants of that place, having the most extensive correspondence, have usually sent them to all parts of the world.

Another account of the origins of these stones is that they are cut at Trier and brought down the Moselle. I could not learn the price of them at the quarry, but I was shown a grindstone of the same stone, five feet in diameter, which cost at Trier six florins. It was of but half the thickness of a millstone. I suppose, therefore, that two millstones would cost about as much as three grindstones.

MOSELLE

The red wines of this country are very indifferent and will not keep.

The best Moselle wines are made about sixty miles from Koblenz, in an excessively mountainous country. The first quality (without any comparison) is that made on the mountain of Brauneberg, and the best crop is that of the Baron Breidbach Burresheim, grand chamberlain and grand bailiff of Koblenz. His receiver, of the name of Mayer, lives at Dusmond. The last fine year was 1783; that wine sells now at fifty louis the *foudre*, which contains six *aumes* of 170 bottles each. This is about twenty-two sous Tournois the bottle. In general, the Baron Burresheim's crops will sell as soon as made, say at the vintage, for 130, 140 and 150 écus the *foudre* (the écus is one and half times the florin of Holland.)

The wine of Wehlen is the second quality and sells new at 120 écus the *foudre*.

Graach-Bispost is the third and sells for about 105 écus. I compared Graach of 1783 with Baron Burresheim's of the same year. The latter is quite clear of acid, stronger and very sensibly the best.

Zeltingen, which sells at 100 écus, is the fourth in quality.

Bernkastel-Kues, the fifth quality, sells at 80 or 90. After this there is a gradation

Florin = 60 Kreuzers
Ecu = 90 Kreuzers

Eighteenth century currency used in Germany

of qualities down to 30 écus. These wines must be five or six years old before they are quite ripe for drinking. The red wines of this country are very indifferent and will not keep.

One thousand plants yield a *foudre* of wine a year in the most plentiful vineyards. In other vineyards it will take 2,000 or 2,500 plants to yield a *foudre*. The culture of 1,000 plants costs about one louis a year. For a day's labor, a man is paid in winter twenty kreuzers (one-third of a florin), in summer twenty-six; a woman's pay is half that.

In the palace of the elector of Trier at Koblenz are large rooms very well warmed by warm air conveyed from an oven below through tubes which open into the rooms. At Koblenz I pass the river on a pendulum boat, and the road to Nassau is over tremendous hills on which are here and there a little corn and more vines; but mostly they are barren. In some of these barren spots are forests of beech and oak, tolerably large, but crooked and knotty. The undergrowth is mostly beech, brush, broom and moss. The soil of the plains and of the hills, where they are cultivable, is reddish.

An oil and vinegar cruet seen in Germany

*H*ESSE

Among the poultry, I have seen no turkeys in Germany
until I arrive in Frankfurt. The stork, or crane,
is very commonly tame here. It is a miserable, dirty, ill-looking bird.

The road from Nassau to Schwalbach is over hills, or rather mountains, both high and steep, always poor and above half of them barren, in beech and oak. At Schwalbach there is some chestnut. Between Schwalbach and Wiesbaden I come in sight of the plains of the Rhine, which are very extensive. From here the lands, both high and low, are very fine and in corn, vines and fruit trees. The country has the appearance of wealth, especially in the approach to Frankfurt.

Among the poultry, I have seen no turkeys in Germany until I arrive in Frankfurt. The stork, or crane, is very commonly tame here. It is a miserable, dirty, ill-looking bird.

The Lutheran faith is the reigning religion here and is equally intolerant to the Catholic and Calvinist faiths, excluding them from the free corps [military].

From Frankfurt to Hanau the road goes through the plains of the Main, which are mulatto and very fine. They are well cultivated till you pass the line between the republic and the landgraviate [territory under the jurisdiction of a count] of Hesse, when you immediately see the effect of the difference of government, notwithstanding the tendency which the neighborhood of such a commercial town as Frankfurt has to counteract the effects of tyranny in its vicinities and to animate them in spite of oppression.

In Frankfurt all is life, bustle and motion. In Hanau there

---

is the silence and quiet of the mansions of the dead. Nobody is seen moving in the streets. Every door is shut. No sound of the saw, the hammer or other utensil of industry. The drum and fife is all that is heard. The streets are cleaner than a German floor because nobody passes through them.

At Williamsbath, near Hanau, is a country seat of the landgrave. There is a ruin which is clever. It presents the remains of an old castle. The ground plan is in the form of a Greek Orthodox cross; the upper story's plan is circular. The four little square towers at the corners finish at the floor of the upper story so as to be only platforms to walk out on. Over the circular room is a platform also, which is covered by a broken parapet which once crowned the top; some of its parts are fallen off, whilst the other parts remain.

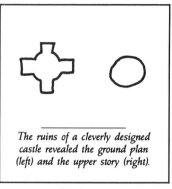

The ruins of a cleverly designed castle revealed the ground plan (left) and the upper story (right).

There is a hermitage in which is a good figure of a hermit in plaster, colored to the life, in the attitude of reading and contemplation and with a table and book before him. In a little cell is his bed, in another his books and some tools. There is a monument erected to the son of the present landgrave, in the form of a pyramid, the base of which is eighteen and a half feet. The side declines from the perpendicular about twenty-one and a half degrees. An arch is carried through it both ways so as present a door in each side. In the middle of this, at the crossing of the two arches, is a marble monument with this inscription: *ante tempus* [before time]. He died at twelve years of age.

Between Hanau and Frankfurt, in sight of the road, is the village of Bergen where was fought the battle of Bergen in the war before last. Things worth noting here are: a folding ladder; the manner of packing china cups and saucers, the former in a circle within the latter; the marks of different manufactures of china; and the top rail of a wagon, which is supported by the washers on the ends of the axletrees.

Because the little tyrants around about have disarmed

their people and made it very criminal to kill game, one knows when the territory of Frankfurt ends by the quality of game which is seen. In Hesse, everybody being allowed to be armed and to hunt on their own lands, there is very little game left in its territory.

The hogs hereabouts resemble extremely the little hog of Virginia, with their small heads and short upright ears. They make the ham of Mainz so much esteemed at Paris.

RHEINGAU-RHEINHESSEN

Though they begin to make wine, as has been said,
at Cologne and continue it up the river indefinitely,
yet it is only from Rudesheim to Hochheim
that wines of the very first quality are made.

I cross the Rhine at Mainz on a bridge 1,840 feet long, supported by forty-seven pontoons. It is not in a direct line, but curved up against the stream, which can strengthen a bridge if the difference between the upper and lower curve is sensible and if the planks of the floor are thick and well jointed together, forming sectors of circles so as to act on the whole as the stones of an arch.

But it has by no means this appearance. Near one end one of the pontoons is allowed to drop downstream some distance with the portion of the bridge's floor belonging to it so as to let a vessel through. Then the pontoon is wound up again into place. To consolidate it the more with the adjoining parts, the loose section is a little higher and has at each end a folding stage which folds back on it when it moves down and when brought up again into place. This whole operation takes but four or five minutes. In the winter the bridge is taken away entirely on account of the ice. And then everything passes on the ice, through the whole winter.

The women do everything here. They dig the earth, plough, saw, cut and split wood, row and tow the boats. In a small but dull kind of boat, with two hands rowing with a kind of large paddle and a square sail, but scarcely a breath of wind, I went down the river at the rate of five miles an hour, making it three and a half hours to Rüdesheim. The wooden barges which go with the current only proceed at one mile and a half an hour. They go night and day.

There are five piers abreast here. Their floats seem to be about eight feet broad. The Rhine yields salmon, carp, pike and perch, and the little rivers running into it yield speckled trout. The plains from Mainz to Rüdesheim are good and in corn. The hills are mostly in vines. The banks of the river are so low that, standing up in the boats, I could generally see what was in the plains. Yet they are seldom overflowed.

Though they begin to make wine, as has been said, at Cologne and continue it up the river indefinitely, yet it is only from Rüdesheim to Hochheim that wines of the very first quality are made. The river happens there to run due east and west, so as to give the hills on that side a southern aspect. And even in this canton, it is only the wines of Hochheim, Johannisberg and Rüdesheim that are considered as the very first quality.

Johannisberg is a little mountain (*berg* signifies mountain), whereon is a religious house, about fifteen miles below Mainz and near the village of Winkel. It has a southern aspect, and its soil is a barren, mulatto clay, mixed with a good deal of stone and some slate. The wine used to be but on a par with that of Hochheim and Rüdesheim, but the place having come to the bishop of Fulda, he improved its culture so as to render it stronger, and since the year 1775 it sells at double the price of the other two. It has none of the acid of the Hochheim and other Rhine wines. There are about sixty *tonneaux* made in a good year, which sell, as soon as of a drinkable age, at 1,000 franks each. The cask here contains seven and a half *aumes* of 170 bottles each.

Rüdesheim is a village about eighteen or twenty miles below Mainz. Its fine wines are made on the hills about a mile below the village, which look to the south, and on the middle and low-

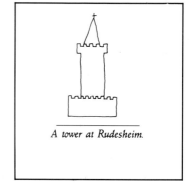

A tower at Rüdesheim.

er parts of them. They are terraced. The soil is gray, about one half of slate and rotten stone, the other half of barren clay. They are excessively steep.

Just behind the village also is a little spot, called Hinder House, belonging to the counts of Sicken and Oschstein, wherein each makes about a *tonneau* of wine of the very first quality. This spot extends from the bottom to the top of the hill. The vignerons of Rüdesheim dung their wines about once in five or six years, putting a one-horse tumbrel [cart] load of dung on every twelve feet square. One thousand plants yield about four *aumes* in a good year. The best crops belong to:

> the canons of Mainz
> the count of Sicken
> the count of Oschstein
> the elector of Mainz
> the count of Meternisch
> Monsieur de Boze
> Monsieur Ackerman, bailiff and innkeeper of
>   Des Trois Couronnes
> Monsieur Ackerman, his son, also
>   of Des Trois Couronnes
> Monsieur Lynn, innkeeper of l'Ange
> the baron of Wetzel
> the Convent of Mariahausen, of the Benedictine
>   order
> Monsieur Johan Yung
> Monsieur de Rieden

These wines begin to be drinkable at about five years old. The proprietors sell them old or young, according to the prices offered and according to their own want of money. There is always a little difference between different casks, and therefore when you choose and buy a single cask, you pay 300, 400, 500 or 600 florins for it. They are not at all acid and to my taste much preferable to Hochheim, though of the same price.

Hochheim is a village about three miles above Mainz on the Main, where it empties into the Rhine. The spot whereon the good wine is made is the hillside from the church down to the plain, a gentle slope of about a quarter of a mile wide and extending half a mile towards Mainz. It is of south-western aspect, very poor, sometimes gray, sometimes mulatto, with a moderate mixture of small broken stone. The vines are planted three feet apart and stuck with sticks about six feet high. They are cut, too, at that height. They are dunged once in three or four years. One thousand plants yield from one *aume* to two *aumes* a year. They begin to yield a little at 3 years old and continue to 100 years, unless sooner killed by a cold winter.

Dick, keeper of the Rothenhaus tavern at Frankfurt, a great wine merchant, who has between 300 and 400 casks of wine in his cellars, tells me that Hochheim of the year 1783 sold, as soon as it was made, at 90 florins the *aume*; Rüdesheim of the same year, as soon as made, at 115 florins; and Markobrunn, at 70 florins. But a peasant of Hochheim tells me that the best crops of Hochheim in the good years, when sold new, sell for only about 32 or 33 florins the *aume* but that it is only the poorer proprietors who sell new.

The fine crops are those of:

Count Ingleheim Baron d'Alberg Count Schimbon the canons of Mainz Counselor Schik de Vetsler the convent of Jacobsber the canon of Fechbach	All of them keep the wine until it is about fifteen years old before they sell it, unless they are offered a very good price sooner.
the Carmelites of Frankfurt	who only sell by the bottle in their own tavern in Frankfurt.
the bailiff of Hochheim	who sells his wine at three or four years old.
Zimmerman, a bourgeois Feldman, a carpenter	and these being poor, they sell new.

Markobrunn (*brunn* signifies a spring and is probably of affinity with the Scottish word *burn*) is a little canton in the same range of hills, adjoining to the village of Hagenheim, about three miles above Johannisberg, subject to the elector of Mainz. It is a sloping hillside of southern aspect, its soil mulatto, poor, and mixed with some stone. This yields wine of the second quality.

On the road between Mainz and Oppenheim are three cantons that are also esteemed as yielding wines of the second quality. These are Laubenheim, Bodenheim and Nierstein.

Laubenheim is a village about four or five miles from Mainz. Its wines are made on a steep hillside, the soil of which is gray, poor, and mixed with some stone. The river there happens to make a short turn to the southeast.

Bodenheim is a village nine miles from Mainz and Nierstein another about ten or eleven miles away. Here, too, the river runs northeast and southwest so as to give the hills between these villages a southeast aspect. Those hills are almost perpendicular, of a vermilion red, and very poor; they have as much rotten stone as earth. It is to be observed that these are the only cantons on the south side of the river which yield good wine, the hills here being generally exposed to the cold winds and turned from the sun.

With respect to the grapes in this country, there are three kinds in use for making white wine — for I take no notice of the red wines, as being absolutely worthless.

The Klemperien [?] grape, of which the inferior qualities of Rhenish wines are made, is cultivated because of its hardness. The wines of this grape descend as low as 100 florins the cask of eight *aumes*.

The riesling grape, which grows only from Hochheim down to Rüdesheim, is small and delicate and succeeds only in this chosen spot. Even at Rüdesheim it yields a fine wine only in the little spot called Hinder House, mentioned before.

The bulk of the good wine, however, is made at Rüdesheim below the village from a the third kind of grape, called the Orleans.

At Oppenheim the plains of the Rhine and Main are united. From that place I see the commencement of the Bergstrasse which separate at first the plains of the Rhine and Main, then cross the Neckar at Heidelberg and form the separation between the plains of the Neckar and Rhine. These plains are sometimes black, sometimes mulatto, and always rich. They are in corn, potatoes and some willows. On the other side again — that is, on the west side — the hills keep at first close to the river. They are about one hundred fifty or two hundred feet high, sloping, red, good and mostly in vines. Above Oppenheim they begin to go off till they join the mountains of Lorraine and Alsace, which separate the waters of the Moselle and Rhine, leaving to the whole valley of the Rhine about twenty or twenty-five miles of breadth.

RHEINPFALZ-BADEN

The gardens at Schwetzingen show how much money may be laid out to make an ugly thing.

There is a bridge over the Rhine at Mannheim supported on thirty-nine pontoons and one over the Neckar on eleven pontoons. The bridge over the Rhine is twenty-one and a half feet wide from rail to rail. The pontoons are four feet deep, fifty-two feet long, and nine feet, eight inches broad. The space between pontoons is eighteen feet, ten inches. From these data the length of the bridge should be 9 ft 8 in + 18 ft 10 in x 40 = 1,140 ft. In order to let vessels pass through, two boats well framed together with their flooring are made to fall downstream together.

Here, too, they make good ham. It is fattened on round potatoes and Indian corn. The farmers smoke what is for their own use in their chimneys. When it is made for sale and in greater quantities than the chimney will hold, they make

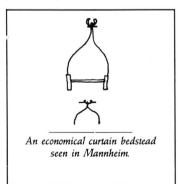

An economical curtain bedstead seen in Mannheim.

the smoke of the chimney pass into an adjoining loft, or apartment, from which it has no issue, and here they hang their hams.

I found an economical curtain bedstead here. The bedstead is seven feet by four feet, two inches. From each leg there goes up an iron rod three-eighths of an inch in diameter. Those from the legs at the foot of the bed meet at top as in the margin, and those from the head meet in like manner, so that the two at the foot form one point and the two at the head another. On these points lies an oval iron rod, whose long diameter is five feet and short one three feet, one inch. There is a hole through this rod at each end, by which it goes on firm on the point of the upright rods. Then a nut screws it down firmly. Ten breadths of stuff, two feet, ten inches wide and eight feet, six inches long, form the curtains. There is no top nor valance. The rings are fastened within two and a half or three inches of the top on the inside, which two and a half or three inches stand up and are an ornament somewhat like a ruffle.

A laborer here receives twenty-four kreuzers per day and feeds himself. One pound of beef sells for eight kreuzers; one pound of mutton or veal, six kreuzers; one pound of pork, seven and a half kreuzers; one pound of fine wheat bread, two kreuzers; and one pound of butter, twenty kreuzers.

There are more soldiers here than other inhabitants, to wit 6,000 soldiers and 4,000 males of full age to the citizens, the whole number of whom is reckoned at 20,000.

The elector placed, in 1768, two males and five females of the Angora goat at Dossenheim, which is at the foot of the mountains. He sold twenty-five last year and has now seventy. They are removed into the mountains sixteen miles beyond Dossenheim.

Heidelberg is on the Neckar just where it issues from the mountains, occupying the first skirt of plain which it forms. The château is up the hill a considerable height. The gardens lie above the château, climbing up the mountain in terraces. This château is the most noble ruin I have ever seen, having been reduced to that state by the French in the time of Louis XIV, 1693. Nothing remains under cover but the chapel. The situation is romantic and pleasing beyond expression. It is on a great scale much like the situation of Petrarch's château at Vaucluse is on a small one.

The famous tun of Heidelberg was built in 1751 and made to contain 30 *foudres* more than the ancient one. It is said to contain 236 *foudres* of 1,200 bottles each. I measured it and found its length external to be twenty feet, three inches. The thickness of the staves is seven and a half inches and the thickness of the hoops seven and a half inches, besides a great deal of external framing. There is no wine in it now.

The gardens at Schwetzingen show how much money may be laid out to make an ugly thing. What is called the English quarter, however, relieves the eye from the straight rows of trees and round and square basins which constitute the great mass of the garden. There are some tolerable morsels of Grecian architecture and a good ruin. The aviary, too, is clever. It consists of cells of about eight feet wide, arranged round, and looking into a circular area of about forty or fifty feet in diameter. The cells have doors both of wire and glass and have small shrubs in them.

The plains of the Rhine on this side are twelve miles wide, bounded by the Bergstrasse. These appear to be eight hundred or one thousand feet high. The lower part is in vines, from which is made what is called the *vin de Nichar*. The upper is in chestnut. There are some cultivated spots, however, quite to the top. The plains are generally mulatto and principally in corn. They are planting potatoes in some parts and leaving others open for maize and tobacco.

Not far from here is an extensive, sandy waste, planted in pine, in which the elector has about two hundred tame sangliers [wild boars]. I saw about fifty; the heaviest, I am told, weigh about three hundred pounds. They are fed on round potatoes and range in the forest of pines. At one village there is a plantation of rhubarb [sold as an astringent], begun in 1769 by a private company. It contains about twenty-five acres and it sometimes employs forty or fifty laborers at a time. The best age to sell the rhubarb is the fifth or sixth year, but the sales being dull, they keep it sometimes to the tenth year. They find it best to let it remain in the ground. They could sell double their current amount if they could find a market. The apothecaries of Frankfurt and of England are the principal buyers.

It is in beds resembling lettuce beds. The plants are four, five or six feet apart. When dug, a thread is passed through every piece of root, and it is hung separate in a kind of rack. When dry, it is rasped; what comes off is given to the cattle.

From Mannheim to Speyer and Karlsruhe the valley preserves its width, extending on each side of the river about ten or twelve miles, but the soil loses much in its quality, becoming sandy and lean, often barren and overgrown with pine thicket.

Between Speyer and Karlsruhe I pass the Rhine in a common skow with oars, where it is between 300 and 400 yards wide. Karlsruhe is the residence of the margrave of Baden, a sovereign prince. His château is built in the midst of a natural forest of several miles in diameter and of the best trees I have seen in these countries. They are mostly oak and would be deemed but indifferent in America. A great deal of money has been spent to do more harm than good to the ground — cutting a number of straight alleys through the forest.

He has pheasants of the gold and silver kinds, the latter very tame, but the former excessively shy. There is also a little enclosure of stone, two and a half feet high and thirty feet in diameter, in which are two tamed beavers. They cannot get over this wall. Within the enclosure there is a pond of fifteen feet in diameter in the center, and at each end there is a little cell for them to retire into, which is stowed with boughs and twigs with leaves on them, which is their principal food. They eat bread also. Twice a week the water is changed.

The town is only an appendage of the château and but a moderate one. I observe they twist the flues of their stoves in any form for ornament merely, without there being any smoke.

Funnels of stoves twisted for ornamental purposes.

As I continue south the valley of the Rhine still preserves its breadth but varies in quality. The culture is generally corn. It is to be noted that through the whole of my route through the Netherlands and the valley of the Rhine, there is a little red clover every here and there. The seed of this is sold to be made into oil.

Within this day or two, the everyday dress of the country women here is black. I have seen no beggars since I entered the territory governed by the margrave of Baden. From Kleve till I entered the margravate of Baden, the roads were strung with beggars — in Hesse the most. The roads are excellent and made so, I presume, out of the coffers of the prince. Elsewhere the road tax has been very heavy. I pay it cheerfully, however, through the territory of Frankfurt and up the Rhine, because fine gravelled roads are kept up. But below Frankfurt the roads are only as made by the carriages, there not appearing to have been ever a day's work employed on them. At Strasbourg I pass the Rhine on a wooden bridge.

FRANCE

*A*LSACE

This wine [vin de paille] *is sought because it is dear,*
while the better wine of Frontignan is rarely seen
at a good table because it is cheap.

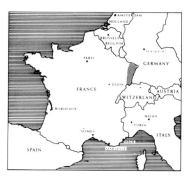

The *vin de paille* is made in the neighborhood of Colmar, in Alsace. It takes its name from the circumstance of spreading the grapes on straw, where they are preserved till spring and then made into wine. The little juice then remaining in them makes a rich, sweet wine, but the dearest in the world without being the best by any means. They charge nine florins the bottle for it in the taverns of Strasbourg. It is the caprice of wealth alone which continues so losing an operation. This wine is sought because it is dear, while the better wine of Frontignan is rarely seen at a good table because it is cheap.

L ORRAINE

The women here, as in Germany, do all sorts of work.
While one considers them as useful and rational companions,
one cannot forget that they are also objects of men's pleasures.
Nor can they ever forget it.

The country between Strasbourg and Nancy is always either mountainous or hilly, red, tolerably good and in small grain. On the hills about Nancy are some small vineyards where a bad wine is made.

The houses, as in Germany, are of scantling, filled in with wicker and mortar and covered either with thatch or tiles. The people, too, here as there, are gathered in villages.

Oxen plough here with collars and hames [side supports for collars]. The awkward figure of their moldboards leads me to consider what should be its form. The function of the moldboard is to receive the sod after the plowshare has cut it and raise it gradually and reverse it. The front end of the moldboard should be horizontal to the intermediate surface, then change gradually from the horizontal to the perpendicular. It should be as wide as the furrow and of a length suited to the construction of the plow.

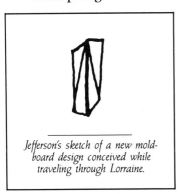

Jefferson's sketch of a new mold-board design conceived while traveling through Lorraine.

The women here, as in Germany, do all sorts of work.

While one considers them as useful and rational companions, one cannot forget that they are also objects of men's pleasures. Nor can they ever forget it. While employed in dirt and drudgery, some tag of a ribbon, some ring, or bit of bracelet, earbob or necklace, or something of that kind, will show that the desire of pleasing is never suspended in them.

It is an honorable circumstance for man that the first moment he is at his ease, he allots the internal employments to his female partner and takes the external on himself. And this circumstance, or its reverse, is a pretty good indication that a people are or are not at their ease. Among the Indians, this indication fails from a particular cause: every Indian man is a soldier or warrior, and the whole body of warriors constitute a standing army, always employed in war or hunting. To support that army there remain no laborers but the women. Here, then, is so heavy a military establishment that the civil part of the nation is reduced to women only. But this is a barbarous perversion of the natural destination of the two sexes. Women are formed by nature for attentions, not for hard labor. A woman never forgets one of the numerous train of little offices which belong to her. A man forgets often.

Nancy is a neat litle town and its environs very agreeable. The valley of the little branch of the Moselle, on which it is, is about a mile wide. The country is very hilly and perhaps a third of it poor and in forest of beech. The other two-thirds is from poor up to middling, red and stony. It is almost entirely in corn, only now and then there are some vines on the hills.

The hills abound with chalk. On all the roads of this day, the rocks coming down from the tops of the hills, at regular intervals like the ribs of an animal, have a very extraordinary appearance. Considerable flocks of sheep and asses and, in the approach to Saint-Dizier, great plantations of apple and cherry trees; here and there a peach tree, all in general bloom. The roads through Lorraine are strung with beggars.

CHAMPAGNE

Their cellars are admirably made. . . .extending into the ground,
in a kind of labyrinth, to a prodigious distance,
with an air hole of two feet in diameter every fifty feet.
I have nowhere seen cellars comparable to these.

The plains of the Marne and Sault uniting appear boundless to the eye until I approach the rivers' confluence at Vitry, where the hills come in on the right. After that the plains are generally only about a mile wide, of middling quality and often stony. Sometimes the ground goes off from the river so sloping that one does not know whether to call it high or low land. The hills are whitish, occasioned by the quantity of chalk which seems to constitute their universal base. They are poor and principally in vines. The streams of water are of the color of milk, occasioned by the chalk also.

Around Épernay the hills abound with chalk. Of this they make lime; it is not so strong as limestone and therefore is to be used in greater proportion. They also cut the blocks into regular forms like stone and build houses of it. The common earth too, well impregnated with this, is made into mortar, molded in the form of brick, and dried in the sun; houses are built of the bricks, which last one hundred or two hundred years. The plains here are a mile wide, red, good, in corn, clover, alfalfa and sainfoin.

The hills are in vines, and this being precisely the canton where the most celebrated wines of Champagne are made, details must be entered into. Remember, however, that they will always relate to the white wines, unless where the red are expressly mentioned. The reason is that their red wines, though much esteemed on the spot, are by no means esteemed elsewhere equally with their white; nor do they merit equal esteem.

The soil is meager, mulatto clay, mixed with small broken stone and a little hue of chalk. It is very dry.

The hills are generally about two hundred and fifty feet high. The good wine is made only in the middle region. The lower region, however, is better than the upper because this last is exposed to cold winds and a colder atmosphere.

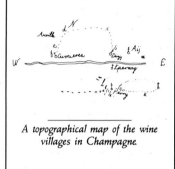

A topographical map of the wine villages in Champagne.

The vines are planted two feet apart. Afterwards they are multiplied. When a stock puts out two shoots, they lay them down, spread them open and cover them with earth, so as to have in the end about a plant for every square foot. For performing this operation they have a special hook nine inches long, which, being stuck in the ground, holds down the main stock while the laborer separates and covers the new shoot.

They leave two buds above the ground. When the vine has shot up enough, they stick it with split sticks of oak, from an inch to an inch and a half square and four feet long, and tie the vine to its stick with a straw. These sticks last forty years. In the fine vineyards, an acre, one year with another, produces about nine *pièces* of 200 bottles each.

They plant the vines in a hole about a foot deep and fill that hole with good mold to make the plant take. Otherwise it would perish. Afterwards, if ever they put dung, it is very little.

During wheat harvest there is a month or six weeks that nothing is done in the vineyards, that is to say, from the first of August to the beginning of vintage. The vintage commences early in September and lasts a month. A laborer in the busiest season earns twenty sous for day's work. In the least busy season he earns fifteen sous.

The bulk of their grapes are purple, which they prefer for making even white wine. They press them very lightly, without treading or permitting them to ferment at all, for about an hour, so that it is the beginning of the running only which makes the bright wine. What follows the beginning is of a straw color and therefore not placed on a level with the first. The last part of the juice, produced by strong pressure, is red and ordinary.

To make wine of the very first quality, they choose the bunches with as much care as if they were to eat. The white grape is preferred, though not as good for wine as the red and more liable to rot in a moist season. It grows better if the soil is excessively poor and therefore, in places with such a soil, is preferred, or rather, is used of necessity because there the red would not grow at all.

The white wines are either *mousseux* (sparkling) or *non-mousseux* (still). The sparkling are little drunk in France but are almost alone known and drunk in foreign countries. This makes so great a demand, and so certain a one, that they endeavor to make all sparkling if they can. This is done by bottling in the spring, from the beginning of March till June.

To make the still wine, they bottle in September. This is only done when they know from some circumstance that the wine will not be sparkling. So if the spring bottling fails to make a sparkling wine, they decant it into other bottles in the fall, and it then makes the very best still wine. In this operation it loses from one-tenth to one-twentieth by sediment. They let it stand in the bottles in this case forty-eight hours with a napkin spread over the mouths, but no cork. The best sparkling wine, decanted in this manner, makes the best still wine; it will keep much longer than that originally made still because it is bottled in September. The sparkling wines lose their briskness the older they are, but they gain in quality with age to a certain length.

These wines are in perfection from two to ten years old and will even be very good to fifteen. Seventeen sixty-six was the best year ever known; 1775 and 1776 next to that; and 1783 was the last good year and that not to be compared with those. These wines stand icing very well.

In Ay Monsieur Dorsay makes 1,000 and 100 *pièces*,

which sell, as soon as made, at 300 florins, and in good years at 400 florins, in the cask. In his cellar I paid to Monsieur Louis, his *homme d'affaires*, for the remains of the year 1783, three florins, ten sous the bottle. Sparkling Champagne of the same degree of excellence would have cost four florins. (The *pièce* and *demiqueue* are the same; the *feuillette* is 100 bottles.)

In Hautvillers the Benedictine monks make 1,000 *pièces*, red and white, but three-fourths red, both of the first quality. The king's table is supplied by them. This enables them to sell at 540 the *pièce*. Though their white is hardly as good as Dorsay's, their red is the best. L' Abbatiale, belonging to the bishop of the place, makes 1,000 to 1,200 *pièces*, red and white (three-fourths red), at 400 to 550 florins because he is a neighbor to the monks.

At Pierry a Monsieur de Casotte makes 500 *pièces*, Monsieur de la Motte, 300 *pièces* and Monsieur de Failli, 300 *pièces*. I tasted his wine of 1779, one of the good years. It was fine, though not equal to Monsieur Dorsay's of 1783.

At Cramant, Avize, Verzy, Mareuil and Verzenay, also, there are some wines of the first quality made. This last place belongs to the Marquis de Sillery. The wines are carried to Sillery and there stored, which is how they come to be called *vins de Sillery*, though not made at Sillery.

All these wines of Épernay and Pierry sell almost as dear as Monsieur Dorsay's, their quality being nearly the same. There are many small proprietors who might make wine of the first quality if they would cull their grapes, but they are too poor for this. Therefore, the proprietors whose names are established buy of the poorer ones the right to cull their vineyards, by which means they increase their quantity, as they find about one-third of the grapes will make wines of the first quality.

The lowest priced wines of all are thirty florins the *pièce*, red or white. They make brandy of the pomace. In very bad years, when their wines become vinegar, they are sold for six florins the *pièce* and made into brandy.

White champagne is deemed good in proportion as it is silky and still. Many circumstances derange the scale of wines. The proprietor of the best vineyard, in the best year, having bad weather come upon him while he is gathering his grapes, makes a bad wine, while his neighbor, holding a more indifferent vineyard, which happens to be in gathering while the weather is good, makes a better.

The Monsieur de Casotte at Pierry formerly held the first house. His successors, by some imperceptible change of culture, have degraded the quality of their wines. Their cellars are admirably made, being about six, eight or ten feet wide, vaulted, and extending into the ground, in a kind of labyrinth, to a prodigious distance, with an air hole of two feet in diameter every fifty feet. From the top of the vault to the surface of the earth is from fifteen to thirty feet. I have nowhere seen cellars comparable to these. In packing their bottles, they lay them on their side; then across them at each end they lay laths and on these another row of bottles. By this means they can take out a bottle from the top or where they want.

From Épernay to Saint-Jean-aux-Bois the road leads over the hills, which in the beginning are indifferent but get better towards the last. The plains, wherever seen, are inconsiderable. After I pass Saint-Jean, the hills become good, and the plains increase. A skirt of a low ridge, which runs in on the extensive plains of the Marne and Seine, is very picturesque. The general bloom of fruit trees proves there are more of them than I had imagined from traveling in other seasons, when they are less distinguishable at a distance from the forest trees.

The type styles selected for this volume were in usage in Thomas Jefferson's era. The main text, for example, was set in Garamond which was designed around 1540 and based on the design of Claude Garamond, a French type founder.

About the Authors

Thomas Jefferson (1743-1826), author of the Declaration of Independence and third President of the United States, wrote the accounts published here during two European journeys he took while serving as U.S. minister to France between 1784-1789.

Dean M. Sagar, who counts Jefferson and wine among his main interests, is a political writer and lobbyist in Washington, D.C., and lives in Jefferson's native Virginia.

About the Editors

James McGrath Morris is editor of Vineyard & Winery Management *magazine and author of* Wineries of the Finger Lakes *(Isidore Stephanus Sons, 1985).*

Persophene Weene is a copy editor who lives and works in Ithaca, N.Y.

For information on books of related interest, or for a catalog of new publications, please write:

Marketing Department
Isidore Stephanus Sons, Publishing
P.O. Box 6772
Ithaca, NY 14851-6772
U.S.A